CHANGE YOUR SHOES

365 *Life Resolutions*

Kathy Andersen

Copyrighted Material

Change Your Shoes ~ 365 Life Resolutions

Copyright © 2015 Katherine (Kathy) Andersen. All Rights Reserved.

No part of this publication may be reproduced, stored in a retrieval system or transmitted, in any form or by any means—electronic, mechanical, photocopying, recording or otherwise—without prior written permission from the publisher, except for the inclusion of brief quotations in a review.

For information about this title or to order other books and/or electronic media, contact the publisher:
KA Connect, LLC
90 Alton Road, Suite 3102
Miami Beach, FL, 33139
www.KathyAndersen.com
books@KathyAndersen.com

ISBN: 978-0-9837126-8-8 (Hardcover). 978-0-9837126-7-1 (Softcover).

Printed in the United States of America

Cover and Interior design: 1106 Design • www.1106design.com

Author Photograph: Javier Valcarcel

~ Introduction ~

Welcome!

You have the power to create the change you want in your life.

My wish for you as you journey through this book, is to take hold of each precious day and use it to create all you want for yourself. Imagine your life after making one resolution to do something for yourself every day!

Often change can seem overwhelming. Yet, the most difficult change starts with a simple step. With each step, one day at a time, you can travel your unique journey to your dreams.

You can do it. Believe it. Commit to it. Don't give up.

Do your best—it is the best you can do. If you miss a day, forgive yourself, and move on the next day.

Enjoy the journey and live your dreams!

Throughout your journey, find resources and ways to share at *www.ChangeYourShoes.com*

Day 1

When we dare to change our shoes, when we are bold enough to step out, when we are brave enough to dig deep, and when we are strong enough to leap high, we can create infinite change. Today, be daring, be brave, be bold, be strong!

MORNING REFLECTION: Date: _____

1. What is your reflection from today's quote?
   _____
   _____

2. Into which shoes do you need to step to move forward in this area of your life?
   _____

3. Out of which shoes do you need to step that hold you back?
   _____

4. What is the one step you can take today to move forward?
   _____

5. Your life resolution for today:
   "I commit to (action) _____ today, as I move closer to experiencing _____ in my life!"

6. With whom will you share today's life resolution to help hold you accountable?
   _____

EVENING REFLECTION:

Which insights will you take into tomorrow?
_____
_____

Day 2

Your intention will guide your reality. Today, declare the intention for your life, and take just one step toward it. Keep intending. Keep taking a step every day!

MORNING REFLECTION: Date: _____

1. What is your reflection from today's quote?
   _____
   _____

2. Into which shoes do you need to step to move forward in this area of your life?
   _____
   _____

3. Out of which shoes do you need to step that hold you back?
   _____
   _____

4. What is the one step you can take today to move forward?
   _____
   _____

5. Your life resolution for today:
   "I commit to (action) _____ today, as I move closer to experiencing _____ in my life!"

6. With whom will you share today's life resolution to help hold you accountable?
   _____

EVENING REFLECTION:

Which insights will you take into tomorrow?
_____
_____

Day 3

We need to pause to discover our space to create, and then choose to start building the landmarks of our lives that are testament to our most purposeful presence. Today, start building your landmarks!

MORNING REFLECTION: Date: _____

1. What is your reflection from today's quote?
   _____
   _____

2. Into which shoes do you need to step to move forward in this area of your life?
   _____

3. Out of which shoes do you need to step that hold you back?
   _____

4. What is the one step you can take today to move forward?
   _____

5. Your life resolution for today:
   "I commit to (action) _____ today, as I move closer to experiencing _____ in my life!"

6. With whom will you share today's life resolution to help hold you accountable?
   _____

EVENING REFLECTION:

Which insights will you take into tomorrow?
_____
_____

Day 4

You can soar to your greatest self on the wings of your soul. Today, allow your soul to soar!

MORNING REFLECTION: Date: _____

1. What is your reflection from today's quote?

2. Into which shoes do you need to step to move forward in this area of your life?

3. Out of which shoes do you need to step that hold you back?

4. What is the one step you can take today to move forward?

5. Your life resolution for today:
   "I commit to (action) _____ today, as I move closer to experiencing _____ in my life!"

6. With whom will you share today's life resolution to help hold you accountable?

EVENING REFLECTION:

Which insights will you take into tomorrow?

Day 5

As a child, I was waiting for someone to come to help.
As an adult I choose to help myself. Today, look
within—all the help you need is there!

MORNING REFLECTION: Date:

1. What is your reflection from today's quote?

2. Into which shoes do you need to step to move forward in this area of your life?

3. Out of which shoes do you need to step that hold you back?

4. What is the one step you can take today to move forward?

5. Your life resolution for today:
   "I commit to (action) _____ today, as I
   move closer to experiencing _____ in my life!"

6. With whom will you share today's life resolution to help hold you accountable?

EVENING REFLECTION:

Which insights will you take into tomorrow?

Day 6

We are the value we place upon ourselves. Today, don't let others de-value you. Set your value and live it!

MORNING REFLECTION: Date: _____

1. What is your reflection from today's quote?

2. Into which shoes do you need to step to move forward in this area of your life?

3. Out of which shoes do you need to step that hold you back?

4. What is the one step you can take today to move forward?

5. Your life resolution for today:
   "I commit to (action) _____ today, as I move closer to experiencing _____ in my life!"

6. With whom will you share today's life resolution to help hold you accountable?

EVENING REFLECTION:

Which insights will you take into tomorrow?

Day 7

Pause and picture all you want in your life: the relationships you want, the financial position you want, the play you want, the work you want, the health you want. Today, take just one step on a path to each.

## MORNING REFLECTION:	Date: _____

1. What is your reflection from today's quote?
   _____
   _____

2. Into which shoes do you need to step to move forward in this area of your life?
   _____
   _____

3. Out of which shoes do you need to step that hold you back?
   _____
   _____

4. What is the one step you can take today to move forward?
   _____
   _____

5. Your life resolution for today:
   "I commit to (action) _____ today, as I
   move closer to experiencing _____ in my life!"

6. With whom will you share today's life resolution to help hold you accountable?
   _____

EVENING REFLECTION:

Which insights will you take into tomorrow?
_____
_____

Day 8

If you allow it, others can take advantage of you.
Today, stand your ground and stand up for you!

MORNING REFLECTION: Date: _____

1. What is your reflection from today's quote?
   _____
   _____

2. Into which shoes do you need to step to move forward in this area of your life?
   _____
   _____

3. Out of which shoes do you need to step that hold you back?
   _____
   _____

4. What is the one step you can take today to move forward?
   _____
   _____

5. Your life resolution for today:
   "I commit to (action) _____ today, as I
   move closer to experiencing _____ in my life!"

6. With whom will you share today's life resolution to help hold you accountable?
   _____

EVENING REFLECTION:

Which insights will you take into tomorrow?
_____
_____

Day 9

We must have hope, belief, and complete determination to do the things most important to us. Today, keep your hope, maintain your belief, and be relentlessly determined!

MORNING REFLECTION: Date: _____

1. What is your reflection from today's quote?
   _____
   _____

2. Into which shoes do you need to step to move forward in this area of your life?
   _____
   _____

3. Out of which shoes do you need to step that hold you back?
   _____
   _____

4. What is the one step you can take today to move forward?
   _____
   _____

5. Your life resolution for today:
   "I commit to (action) _____ today, as I move closer to experiencing _____ in my life!"

6. With whom will you share today's life resolution to help hold you accountable?

EVENING REFLECTION:

Which insights will you take into tomorrow?
_____
_____

Day 10

Without the honest and uninhibited search for that which is deep within us, the search for that which is around us can only be superficial and frivolous. Today, search inside yourself!

MORNING REFLECTION: Date: _____

1. What is your reflection from today's quote?
   _____
   _____

2. Into which shoes do you need to step to move forward in this area of your life?
   _____
   _____

3. Out of which shoes do you need to step that hold you back?
   _____
   _____

4. What is the one step you can take today to move forward?
   _____
   _____

5. Your life resolution for today:
   "I commit to (action) _____ today, as I move closer to experiencing _____ in my life!"

6. With whom will you share today's life resolution to help hold you accountable?
   _____

EVENING REFLECTION:

Which insights will you take into tomorrow?
_____
_____

Day 11

We are not limited by what we have been.
We are unlimited by what we can become. Today, become!

MORNING REFLECTION: Date: _____

1. What is your reflection from today's quote?
   _____
   _____

2. Into which shoes do you need to step to move forward in this area of your life?
   _____
   _____

3. Out of which shoes do you need to step that hold you back?
   _____
   _____

4. What is the one step you can take today to move forward?
   _____
   _____

5. Your life resolution for today:
   "I commit to (action) _____ today, as I move closer to experiencing _____ in my life!"

6. With whom will you share today's life resolution to help hold you accountable?
   _____

EVENING REFLECTION:

Which insights will you take into tomorrow?
_____
_____

Day 12

Amidst your uncertainty, there is light that will guide you. Today, see your light, and be guided.

MORNING REFLECTION: Date: _____

1. What is your reflection from today's quote?
   _____
   _____

2. Into which shoes do you need to step to move forward in this area of your life?
   _____
   _____

3. Out of which shoes do you need to step that hold you back?
   _____
   _____

4. What is the one step you can take today to move forward?
   _____
   _____

5. Your life resolution for today:
   "I commit to (action) _____ today, as I move closer to experiencing _____ in my life!"

6. With whom will you share today's life resolution to help hold you accountable?
   _____

EVENING REFLECTION:

Which insights will you take into tomorrow?
_____
_____

Day 13

"All I have is me" can be your greatest thought.
Today, be your "all!"

MORNING REFLECTION: Date: _____

1. What is your reflection from today's quote?
   _____
   _____

2. Into which shoes do you need to step to move forward in this area of your life?
   _____
   _____

3. Out of which shoes do you need to step that hold you back?
   _____
   _____

4. What is the one step you can take today to move forward?
   _____
   _____

5. Your life resolution for today:
   "I commit to (action) _____ today, as I move closer to experiencing _____ in my life!"

6. With whom will you share today's life resolution to help hold you accountable?
   _____

EVENING REFLECTION:

Which insights will you take into tomorrow?
_____

Day 14

Don't settle for less, when you are so much more.
Today, remind yourself how much you are!

MORNING REFLECTION: Date: _____

1. What is your reflection from today's quote?
   _____
   _____

2. Into which shoes do you need to step to move forward in this area of your life?
   _____
   _____

3. Out of which shoes do you need to step that hold you back?
   _____
   _____

4. What is the one step you can take today to move forward?
   _____
   _____

5. Your life resolution for today:
   "I commit to (action) _____ today, as I
   move closer to experiencing _____ in my life!"

6. With whom will you share today's life resolution to help hold you accountable?
   _____

EVENING REFLECTION:

Which insights will you take into tomorrow?
_____
_____

Day 15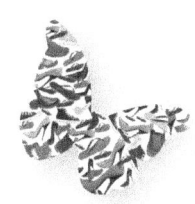

With our thoughts and intentions, we can change our
reality. Today, don't hold back from the change you want
in your life. Think it, intend it, and leap into it!

MORNING REFLECTION: Date: _____

1. What is your reflection from today's quote?
   _____
   _____

2. Into which shoes do you need to step to move forward in this area of your life?
   _____
   _____

3. Out of which shoes do you need to step that hold you back?
   _____
   _____

4. What is the one step you can take today to move forward?
   _____
   _____

5. Your life resolution for today:
   "I commit to (action) _____ today, as I
   move closer to experiencing _____ in my life!"

6. With whom will you share today's life resolution to help hold you accountable?
   _____

EVENING REFLECTION:

Which insights will you take into tomorrow?
_____
_____

Day 16

Keep filling yourself with the fuel to chase your dreams.
Today, pause, re-fuel, and don't let your dreams escape you!

MORNING REFLECTION: Date: _____

1. What is your reflection from today's quote?
   _____
   _____

2. Into which shoes do you need to step to move forward in this area of your life?
   _____
   _____

3. Out of which shoes do you need to step that hold you back?
   _____
   _____

4. What is the one step you can take today to move forward?
   _____
   _____

5. Your life resolution for today:
   "I commit to (action) _____ today, as I move closer to experiencing _____ in my life!"

6. With whom will you share today's life resolution to help hold you accountable?
   _____

EVENING REFLECTION:

Which insights will you take into tomorrow?
_____
_____

Day 17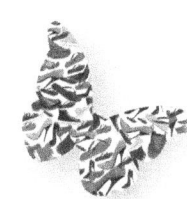

Peace is a stream that flows within us.
Today, let it flow through you and out to those around you.

MORNING REFLECTION: Date: _____

1. What is your reflection from today's quote?
   _____

2. Into which shoes do you need to step to move forward in this area of your life?
   _____

3. Out of which shoes do you need to step that hold you back?
   _____

4. What is the one step you can take today to move forward?
   _____

5. Your life resolution for today:
   "I commit to (action) _____ today, as I
   move closer to experiencing _____ in my life!"

6. With whom will you share today's life resolution to help hold you accountable?
   _____

EVENING REFLECTION:

Which insights will you take into tomorrow?
_____

Day 18

There are so many things we leave unsaid. Today, share the one thing you would most like to share with those you love.

MORNING REFLECTION: Date: _____

1. What is your reflection from today's quote?

2. Into which shoes do you need to step to move forward in this area of your life?

3. Out of which shoes do you need to step that hold you back?

4. What is the one step you can take today to move forward?

5. Your life resolution for today:
   "I commit to (action) _____ today, as I move closer to experiencing _____ in my life!"

6. With whom will you share today's life resolution to help hold you accountable?

EVENING REFLECTION:

Which insights will you take into tomorrow?

Day 19

You have infinite and divine power to rise above your challenges,
and into the light of all you are here to be. Today, rise and be!

MORNING REFLECTION: Date: _____

1. What is your reflection from today's quote?
   _____
   _____

2. Into which shoes do you need to step to move forward in this area of your life?
   _____

3. Out of which shoes do you need to step that hold you back?
   _____

4. What is the one step you can take today to move forward?
   _____

5. Your life resolution for today:
   "I commit to (action) _____ today, as I
   move closer to experiencing _____ in my life!"

6. With whom will you share today's life resolution to help hold you accountable?
   _____

EVENING REFLECTION:

Which insights will you take into tomorrow?
_____
_____

Day 20

In our relentless pursuits, impatience can make us leap in the wrong direction. Today, allow patience to be your guide.

MORNING REFLECTION: Date: _____

1. What is your reflection from today's quote?
   _____
   _____

2. Into which shoes do you need to step to move forward in this area of your life?
   _____
   _____

3. Out of which shoes do you need to step that hold you back?
   _____
   _____

4. What is the one step you can take today to move forward?
   _____
   _____

5. Your life resolution for today:
   "I commit to (action) _____ today, as I move closer to experiencing _____ in my life!"

6. With whom will you share today's life resolution to help hold you accountable?
   _____

EVENING REFLECTION:

Which insights will you take into tomorrow?
_____
_____

Day 21
You have choices. Today, choose!

MORNING REFLECTION: Date:

1. What is your reflection from today's quote?

2. Into which shoes do you need to step to move forward in this area of your life?

3. Out of which shoes do you need to step that hold you back?

4. What is the one step you can take today to move forward?

5. Your life resolution for today:
   "I commit to (action) _____ today, as I move closer to experiencing _____ in my life!"

6. With whom will you share today's life resolution to help hold you accountable?

EVENING REFLECTION:

Which insights will you take into tomorrow?

Day 22

Honor the choice you have to accept no less than you fully desire. Today, reject less.

MORNING REFLECTION: Date:

1. What is your reflection from today's quote?

2. Into which shoes do you need to step to move forward in this area of your life?

3. Out of which shoes do you need to step that hold you back?

4. What is the one step you can take today to move forward?

5. Your life resolution for today:
   "I commit to (action) _____ today, as I move closer to experiencing _____ in my life!"

6. With whom will you share today's life resolution to help hold you accountable?

EVENING REFLECTION:

Which insights will you take into tomorrow?

Day 23

Don't hold yourself back—you are the only who can.
Today, seize your power and defy those who would take it.

MORNING REFLECTION: Date: _____

1. What is your reflection from today's quote?
   _____
   _____

2. Into which shoes do you need to step to move forward in this area of your life?
   _____

3. Out of which shoes do you need to step that hold you back?
   _____

4. What is the one step you can take today to move forward?
   _____

5. Your life resolution for today:
   "I commit to (action) _____ today, as I
   move closer to experiencing _____ in my life!"

6. With whom will you share today's life resolution to help hold you accountable?
   _____

EVENING REFLECTION:

Which insights will you take into tomorrow?
_____
_____

Day 24

In our busyness, our lives can become a maze. Today, step out of the maze of your life and see your bigger picture.

MORNING REFLECTION: Date: _____

1. What is your reflection from today's quote?
   _____
   _____

2. Into which shoes do you need to step to move forward in this area of your life?
   _____
   _____

3. Out of which shoes do you need to step that hold you back?
   _____
   _____

4. What is the one step you can take today to move forward?
   _____
   _____

5. Your life resolution for today:
   "I commit to (action) _____ today, as I move closer to experiencing _____ in my life!"

6. With whom will you share today's life resolution to help hold you accountable?
   _____

EVENING REFLECTION:

Which insights will you take into tomorrow?
_____
_____

Day 25

Within us is the spirit that will set us free.
Today, release your spirit into your world. Be free to be.

MORNING REFLECTION: Date: _____

1. What is your reflection from today's quote?

2. Into which shoes do you need to step to move forward in this area of your life?

3. Out of which shoes do you need to step that hold you back?

4. What is the one step you can take today to move forward?

5. Your life resolution for today:
   "I commit to (action) _____ today, as I move closer to experiencing _____ in my life!"

6. With whom will you share today's life resolution to help hold you accountable?

EVENING REFLECTION:

Which insights will you take into tomorrow?

Day 26

The door to our dreams is before us in each moment. Today, pause to see it, and step into the power of all you are here to be.

MORNING REFLECTION: Date: _____

1. What is your reflection from today's quote?

2. Into which shoes do you need to step to move forward in this area of your life?

3. Out of which shoes do you need to step that hold you back?

4. What is the one step you can take today to move forward?

5. Your life resolution for today:
   "I commit to (action) _____ today, as I move closer to experiencing _____ in my life!"

6. With whom will you share today's life resolution to help hold you accountable?

EVENING REFLECTION:

Which insights will you take into tomorrow?

Day 27

With each drop of change, we can create oceans. Today, be the
drop in the ocean that will tip the change in the world!

MORNING REFLECTION: Date: _____

1. What is your reflection from today's quote?
   _____
   _____

2. Into which shoes do you need to step to move forward in this area of your life?
   _____
   _____

3. Out of which shoes do you need to step that hold you back?
   _____
   _____

4. What is the one step you can take today to move forward?
   _____
   _____

5. Your life resolution for today:
   "I commit to (action) _____ today, as I
   move closer to experiencing _____ in my life!"

6. With whom will you share today's life resolution to help hold you accountable?
   _____

EVENING REFLECTION:

Which insights will you take into tomorrow?
_____
_____

Day 28

Dare to be the greatest you can be. Don't allow anyone to steal that power from you. Today, dare to be great!

MORNING REFLECTION: Date: _____

1. What is your reflection from today's quote?
   _____
   _____

2. Into which shoes do you need to step to move forward in this area of your life?
   _____
   _____

3. Out of which shoes do you need to step that hold you back?
   _____
   _____

4. What is the one step you can take today to move forward?
   _____
   _____

5. Your life resolution for today:
   "I commit to (action) _____ today, as I move closer to experiencing _____ in my life!"

6. With whom will you share today's life resolution to help hold you accountable?
   _____

EVENING REFLECTION:

Which insights will you take into tomorrow?
_____
_____

Day 29

Your random act of kindness will change the life of
another, and your own. Today, be kind.

MORNING REFLECTION: Date: _____

1. What is your reflection from today's quote?
   _____
   _____

2. Into which shoes do you need to step to move forward in this area of your life?
   _____
   _____

3. Out of which shoes do you need to step that hold you back?
   _____
   _____

4. What is the one step you can take today to move forward?
   _____
   _____

5. Your life resolution for today:
   "I commit to (action) _____ today, as I
   move closer to experiencing _____ in my life!"

6. With whom will you share today's life resolution to help hold you accountable?
   _____

EVENING REFLECTION:

Which insights will you take into tomorrow?
_____
_____

Day 30

Is where you stand, where you want to be? Today, take a moment to feel the answer from the depths of your soul, and then step into where you want to be standing in your life.

MORNING REFLECTION: Date: _____

1. What is your reflection from today's quote?
   _____
   _____

2. Into which shoes do you need to step to move forward in this area of your life?
   _____
   _____

3. Out of which shoes do you need to step that hold you back?
   _____
   _____

4. What is the one step you can take today to move forward?
   _____
   _____

5. Your life resolution for today:
   "I commit to (action) _____ today, as I move closer to experiencing _____ in my life!"

6. With whom will you share today's life resolution to help hold you accountable?
   _____

EVENING REFLECTION:

Which insights will you take into tomorrow?
_____
_____

Day 31

Look at your life from a higher perspective.
Today, see new paths and step onto them.

MORNING REFLECTION: Date:

1. What is your reflection from today's quote?

2. Into which shoes do you need to step to move forward in this area of your life?

3. Out of which shoes do you need to step that hold you back?

4. What is the one step you can take today to move forward?

5. Your life resolution for today:
   "I commit to (action) _____ today, as I move closer to experiencing _____ in my life!"

6. With whom will you share today's life resolution to help hold you accountable?

EVENING REFLECTION:

Which insights will you take into tomorrow?

Day 32

Follow your path, but rest along the way.
Today, listen to your inner needs.

MORNING REFLECTION: Date: _____

1. What is your reflection from today's quote?
   _____
   _____

2. Into which shoes do you need to step to move forward in this area of your life?
   _____

3. Out of which shoes do you need to step that hold you back?
   _____

4. What is the one step you can take today to move forward?
   _____

5. Your life resolution for today:
   "I commit to (action) _____ today, as I
   move closer to experiencing _____ in my life!"

6. With whom will you share today's life resolution to help hold you accountable?
   _____

EVENING REFLECTION:

Which insights will you take into tomorrow?
_____
_____

Day 33

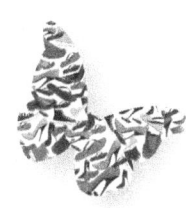

As a child, I didn't know I had a choice. As an adult,
I hold my power to choose as the most precious gift we have.
Today, live in the power of your choices.

MORNING REFLECTION: Date:

1. What is your reflection from today's quote?

2. Into which shoes do you need to step to move forward in this area of your life?

3. Out of which shoes do you need to step that hold you back?

4. What is the one step you can take today to move forward?

5. Your life resolution for today:
   "I commit to (action) _____ today, as I move closer to experiencing _____ in my life!"

6. With whom will you share today's life resolution to help hold you accountable?

EVENING REFLECTION:

Which insights will you take into tomorrow?

Day 34

When you feel struggle, dig deep to find the seed of your higher self within you, and water it until it blooms. Today, allow growth to come from your tears.

MORNING REFLECTION: Date: _____

1. What is your reflection from today's quote?

2. Into which shoes do you need to step to move forward in this area of your life?

3. Out of which shoes do you need to step that hold you back?

4. What is the one step you can take today to move forward?

5. Your life resolution for today:
   "I commit to (action) _____ today, as I move closer to experiencing _____ in my life!"

6. With whom will you share today's life resolution to help hold you accountable?

EVENING REFLECTION:

Which insights will you take into tomorrow?

Day 35

Choose to be happy.
Today, turn your darkness into brightness!

MORNING REFLECTION: Date: _____

1. What is your reflection from today's quote?
   _____
   _____

2. Into which shoes do you need to step to move forward in this area of your life?
   _____
   _____

3. Out of which shoes do you need to step that hold you back?
   _____
   _____

4. What is the one step you can take today to move forward?
   _____
   _____

5. Your life resolution for today:
   "I commit to (action) _____ today, as I
   move closer to experiencing _____ in my life!"

6. With whom will you share today's life resolution to help hold you accountable?
   _____

EVENING REFLECTION:

Which insights will you take into tomorrow?
_____
_____

Day 36

The simplicity of our lives is love.
Today, simply love.

MORNING REFLECTION: Date: _____

1. What is your reflection from today's quote?
   _____
   _____

2. Into which shoes do you need to step to move forward in this area of your life?
   _____

3. Out of which shoes do you need to step that hold you back?
   _____

4. What is the one step you can take today to move forward?
   _____

5. Your life resolution for today:
   "I commit to (action) _____ today, as I
   move closer to experiencing _____ in my life!"

6. With whom will you share today's life resolution to help hold you accountable?
   _____

EVENING REFLECTION:

Which insights will you take into tomorrow?
_____

Day 37

The day is here for you to leap into life.
Today, leap!

MORNING REFLECTION: Date: _____

1. What is your reflection from today's quote?
   _____
   _____

2. Into which shoes do you need to step to move forward in this area of your life?
   _____
   _____

3. Out of which shoes do you need to step that hold you back?
   _____
   _____

4. What is the one step you can take today to move forward?
   _____
   _____

5. Your life resolution for today:
   "I commit to (action) _____ today, as I
   move closer to experiencing _____ in my life!"

6. With whom will you share today's life resolution to help hold you accountable?
   _____

EVENING REFLECTION:

Which insights will you take into tomorrow?
_____
_____

Day 38

In this moment, remember, you have life. Today, love it, embrace it, cherish it, express it, live it!

MORNING REFLECTION: Date: _____

1. What is your reflection from today's quote?

2. Into which shoes do you need to step to move forward in this area of your life?

3. Out of which shoes do you need to step that hold you back?

4. What is the one step you can take today to move forward?

5. Your life resolution for today:
   "I commit to (action) _____ today, as I move closer to experiencing _____ in my life!"

6. With whom will you share today's life resolution to help hold you accountable?

EVENING REFLECTION:

Which insights will you take into tomorrow?

Day 39

We are each full of brilliance and life that is ageless and timeless. Today, let it shine!

MORNING REFLECTION: Date: _____

1. What is your reflection from today's quote?
   _____
   _____

2. Into which shoes do you need to step to move forward in this area of your life?
   _____
   _____

3. Out of which shoes do you need to step that hold you back?
   _____
   _____

4. What is the one step you can take today to move forward?
   _____
   _____

5. Your life resolution for today:
   "I commit to (action) _____ today, as I move closer to experiencing _____ in my life!"

6. With whom will you share today's life resolution to help hold you accountable?
   _____

EVENING REFLECTION:

Which insights will you take into tomorrow?
_____
_____

Day 40

We are as grand as the grandest landscapes. Today, allow the grandeur around you to awaken all that is within you.

MORNING REFLECTION: Date: _____

1. What is your reflection from today's quote?
   _____
   _____

2. Into which shoes do you need to step to move forward in this area of your life?
   _____
   _____

3. Out of which shoes do you need to step that hold you back?
   _____
   _____

4. What is the one step you can take today to move forward?
   _____
   _____

5. Your life resolution for today:
   "I commit to (action) _____ today, as I move closer to experiencing _____ in my life!"

6. With whom will you share today's life resolution to help hold you accountable?
   _____

EVENING REFLECTION:

Which insights will you take into tomorrow?
_____
_____

Day 41

The day is waiting for you to take a break.
Today, take it!

MORNING REFLECTION: Date: _____

1. What is your reflection from today's quote?

2. Into which shoes do you need to step to move forward in this area of your life?

3. Out of which shoes do you need to step that hold you back?

4. What is the one step you can take today to move forward?

5. Your life resolution for today:
   "I commit to (action) _____ today, as I move closer to experiencing _____ in my life!"

6. With whom will you share today's life resolution to help hold you accountable?

EVENING REFLECTION:

Which insights will you take into tomorrow?

Day 42

Our lives can become like merry-go-rounds spinning too fast.
Today, take the controls, and ride at your own pace.

MORNING REFLECTION: Date: _____

1. What is your reflection from today's quote?

2. Into which shoes do you need to step to move forward in this area of your life?

3. Out of which shoes do you need to step that hold you back?

4. What is the one step you can take today to move forward?

5. Your life resolution for today:
   "I commit to (action) _____ today, as I move closer to experiencing _____ in my life!"

6. With whom will you share today's life resolution to help hold you accountable?

EVENING REFLECTION:

Which insights will you take into tomorrow?

Day 43

Follow your path. Today, take a step and go!

MORNING REFLECTION: Date: _____

1. What is your reflection from today's quote?
   _____
   _____

2. Into which shoes do you need to step to move forward in this area of your life?
   _____
   _____

3. Out of which shoes do you need to step that hold you back?
   _____
   _____

4. What is the one step you can take today to move forward?
   _____
   _____

5. Your life resolution for today:
   "I commit to (action) _____ today, as I move closer to experiencing _____ in my life!"

6. With whom will you share today's life resolution to help hold you accountable?
   _____

EVENING REFLECTION:

Which insights will you take into tomorrow?
_____
_____

Day 44

To reach the heights of your life, you must take one step each day and step higher. Today, simply take that step and allow the rest to happen.

MORNING REFLECTION: Date: _____

1. What is your reflection from today's quote?
   _____
   _____

2. Into which shoes do you need to step to move forward in this area of your life?
   _____
   _____

3. Out of which shoes do you need to step that hold you back?
   _____
   _____

4. What is the one step you can take today to move forward?
   _____
   _____

5. Your life resolution for today:
   "I commit to (action) _____ today, as I move closer to experiencing _____ in my life!"

6. With whom will you share today's life resolution to help hold you accountable?
   _____

EVENING REFLECTION:

Which insights will you take into tomorrow?
   _____
   _____

Day 45

With the choices before you, look above and beyond as you contemplate to where you wish to fly. Today, choose your flight path!

MORNING REFLECTION: Date: _____

1. What is your reflection from today's quote?
   _____
   _____

2. Into which shoes do you need to step to move forward in this area of your life?
   _____
   _____

3. Out of which shoes do you need to step that hold you back?
   _____
   _____

4. What is the one step you can take today to move forward?
   _____
   _____

5. Your life resolution for today:
   "I commit to (action) _____ today, as I move closer to experiencing _____ in my life!"

6. With whom will you share today's life resolution to help hold you accountable?
   _____

EVENING REFLECTION:

Which insights will you take into tomorrow?
_____
_____

Day 46

We can be born anew each day. We can rise to the highest state of our being, and create our brightest and most powerful lives. Today, shine anew!

MORNING REFLECTION: Date: _____

1. What is your reflection from today's quote?
   _____
   _____

2. Into which shoes do you need to step to move forward in this area of your life?
   _____

3. Out of which shoes do you need to step that hold you back?
   _____

4. What is the one step you can take today to move forward?
   _____

5. Your life resolution for today:
   "I commit to (action) _____ today, as I move closer to experiencing _____ in my life!"

6. With whom will you share today's life resolution to help hold you accountable?
   _____

EVENING REFLECTION:

Which insights will you take into tomorrow?
_____

Day 47

Every day we have the chance to hold love in our hands.
Today, reach out, reach in, and love.

MORNING REFLECTION: Date: _____

1. What is your reflection from today's quote?
   _____
   _____

2. Into which shoes do you need to step to move forward in this area of your life?
   _____
   _____

3. Out of which shoes do you need to step that hold you back?
   _____
   _____

4. What is the one step you can take today to move forward?
   _____
   _____

5. Your life resolution for today:
   "I commit to (action) _____ today, as I move closer to experiencing _____ in my life!"

6. With whom will you share today's life resolution to help hold you accountable?
   _____

EVENING REFLECTION:

Which insights will you take into tomorrow?
_____
_____

Day 48

When you are not sure how to take the next step forward, look to the gifts within you. Today, allow your inner gifts to guide you.

MORNING REFLECTION: Date: _____

1. What is your reflection from today's quote?
   _____
   _____

2. Into which shoes do you need to step to move forward in this area of your life?
   _____

3. Out of which shoes do you need to step that hold you back?
   _____

4. What is the one step you can take today to move forward?
   _____

5. Your life resolution for today:
   "I commit to (action) _____ today, as I move closer to experiencing _____ in my life!"

6. With whom will you share today's life resolution to help hold you accountable?
   _____

EVENING REFLECTION:

Which insights will you take into tomorrow?
_____

Day 49

When we share a piece of ourselves with another, we
create the opportunity to grow and blossom. Today, allow
a connection with another to bloom in your life.

MORNING REFLECTION: Date: _____

1. What is your reflection from today's quote?
   _____
   _____

2. Into which shoes do you need to step to move forward in this area of your life?
   _____
   _____

3. Out of which shoes do you need to step that hold you back?
   _____
   _____

4. What is the one step you can take today to move forward?
   _____
   _____

5. Your life resolution for today:
   "I commit to (action) _____ today, as I
   move closer to experiencing _____ in my life!"

6. With whom will you share today's life resolution to help hold you accountable?
   _____

EVENING REFLECTION:

Which insights will you take into tomorrow?
_____

Day 50

We each have a powerful force of nature within us.
Strong, calm, powerful, wise, protecting, nurturing, ready.
Pause and renew in the power resting and waiting within you.

MORNING REFLECTION: Date: _____

1. What is your reflection from today's quote?
   _____
   _____

2. Into which shoes do you need to step to move forward in this area of your life?
   _____
   _____

3. Out of which shoes do you need to step that hold you back?
   _____
   _____

4. What is the one step you can take today to move forward?
   _____
   _____

5. Your life resolution for today:
   "I commit to (action) _____ today, as I move closer to experiencing _____ in my life!"

6. With whom will you share today's life resolution to help hold you accountable?
   _____

EVENING REFLECTION:

Which insights will you take into tomorrow?
_____

Day 51

As you awaken into your day, awaken into the beauty of
your being. Today, glow in your beautiful being!

MORNING REFLECTION: Date: _____

1. What is your reflection from today's quote?

2. Into which shoes do you need to step to move forward in this area of your life?

3. Out of which shoes do you need to step that hold you back?

4. What is the one step you can take today to move forward?

5. Your life resolution for today:
   "I commit to (action) _____ today, as I move closer to experiencing _____ in my life!"

6. With whom will you share today's life resolution to help hold you accountable?

EVENING REFLECTION:

Which insights will you take into tomorrow?

Day 52

Don't settle for less when you are here to be more!
Today, be more.

MORNING REFLECTION: Date: _____

1. What is your reflection from today's quote?
   _____
   _____

2. Into which shoes do you need to step to move forward in this area of your life?
   _____
   _____

3. Out of which shoes do you need to step that hold you back?
   _____
   _____

4. What is the one step you can take today to move forward?
   _____
   _____

5. Your life resolution for today:
   "I commit to (action) _____ today, as I
   move closer to experiencing _____ in my life!"

6. With whom will you share today's life resolution to help hold you accountable?
   _____

EVENING REFLECTION:

Which insights will you take into tomorrow?
_____

Day 53

In our tranquil retreats, we can allow peace and
clarity to emerge. Today, take time to retreat!

MORNING REFLECTION: Date: _____

1. What is your reflection from today's quote?
   _____
   _____

2. Into which shoes do you need to step to move forward in this area of your life?
   _____
   _____

3. Out of which shoes do you need to step that hold you back?
   _____
   _____

4. What is the one step you can take today to move forward?
   _____
   _____

5. Your life resolution for today:
   "I commit to (action) _____ today, as I
   move closer to experiencing _____ in my life!"

6. With whom will you share today's life resolution to help hold you accountable?

EVENING REFLECTION:

Which insights will you take into tomorrow?
   _____
   _____

Day 54

In every moment, doors await us.
Today, choose just one, and open it!

MORNING REFLECTION: Date: _____

1. What is your reflection from today's quote?
   _____
   _____

2. Into which shoes do you need to step to move forward in this area of your life?
   _____
   _____

3. Out of which shoes do you need to step that hold you back?
   _____
   _____

4. What is the one step you can take today to move forward?
   _____
   _____

5. Your life resolution for today:
   "I commit to (action) _____ today, as I
   move closer to experiencing _____ in my life!"

6. With whom will you share today's life resolution to help hold you accountable?
   _____

EVENING REFLECTION:

Which insights will you take into tomorrow?
_____
_____

Day 55

We are each created as magical beings, able to transform
into the shape and color we wish to be in our lives.
Today, choose your shape and color.

MORNING REFLECTION: Date: _____

1. What is your reflection from today's quote?
   _____
   _____

2. Into which shoes do you need to step to move forward in this area of your life?
   _____
   _____

3. Out of which shoes do you need to step that hold you back?
   _____
   _____

4. What is the one step you can take today to move forward?
   _____
   _____

5. Your life resolution for today:
   "I commit to (action) _____ today, as I
   move closer to experiencing _____ in my life!"

6. With whom will you share today's life resolution to help hold you accountable?
   _____

EVENING REFLECTION:

Which insights will you take into tomorrow?
_____

Day 56

Our days will sometimes present us with rain and thunderstorms. Yet, we can shield ourselves with the colors we choose to bring into our day. Today, stay in the color in your life!

MORNING REFLECTION: Date: _____

1. What is your reflection from today's quote?

2. Into which shoes do you need to step to move forward in this area of your life?

3. Out of which shoes do you need to step that hold you back?

4. What is the one step you can take today to move forward?

5. Your life resolution for today:
   "I commit to (action) _____ today, as I move closer to experiencing _____ in my life!"

6. With whom will you share today's life resolution to help hold you accountable?

EVENING REFLECTION:

Which insights will you take into tomorrow?

Day 57

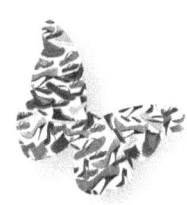

The paths we wish to travel in our lives are often clearer when we elevate ourselves and see our lives from a higher platform. Today, elevate yourself, see the paths you desire, and follow them.

MORNING REFLECTION: Date: _____

1. What is your reflection from today's quote?
   _____
   _____

2. Into which shoes do you need to step to move forward in this area of your life?
   _____
   _____

3. Out of which shoes do you need to step that hold you back?
   _____
   _____

4. What is the one step you can take today to move forward?
   _____
   _____

5. Your life resolution for today:
   "I commit to (action) _____ today, as I move closer to experiencing _____ in my life!"

6. With whom will you share today's life resolution to help hold you accountable?
   _____

EVENING REFLECTION:

Which insights will you take into tomorrow?
_____
_____

Day 58
Love is. Today, show someone you love some love!

MORNING REFLECTION: Date: _____

1. What is your reflection from today's quote?

2. Into which shoes do you need to step to move forward in this area of your life?

3. Out of which shoes do you need to step that hold you back?

4. What is the one step you can take today to move forward?

5. Your life resolution for today:
   "I commit to (action) _____ today, as I move closer to experiencing _____ in my life!"

6. With whom will you share today's life resolution to help hold you accountable?

EVENING REFLECTION:
Which insights will you take into tomorrow?

Day 59

The stepping stones that lead us to our greatest horizons are often laid out before us. We just need to see them and take the step. Today, step onto the stones before you!

MORNING REFLECTION: Date: _____

1. What is your reflection from today's quote?
   _____
   _____

2. Into which shoes do you need to step to move forward in this area of your life?
   _____
   _____

3. Out of which shoes do you need to step that hold you back?
   _____
   _____

4. What is the one step you can take today to move forward?
   _____
   _____

5. Your life resolution for today:
   "I commit to (action) _____ today, as I move closer to experiencing _____ in my life!"

6. With whom will you share today's life resolution to help hold you accountable?
   _____

EVENING REFLECTION:

Which insights will you take into tomorrow?
_____
_____

Day 60

When we pause and stand "barefoot" in our lives,
we can choose the shoes we will wear to move us forward.
Today, choose the shoes you love!

MORNING REFLECTION: Date: _____

1. What is your reflection from today's quote?
   _____
   _____

2. Into which shoes do you need to step to move forward in this area of your life?
   _____
   _____

3. Out of which shoes do you need to step that hold you back?
   _____
   _____

4. What is the one step you can take today to move forward?
   _____
   _____

5. Your life resolution for today:
   "I commit to (action) _____ today, as I
   move closer to experiencing _____ in my life!"

6. With whom will you share today's life resolution to help hold you accountable?
   _____

EVENING REFLECTION:

Which insights will you take into tomorrow?
_____
_____

Day 61

The abundance within you is waiting for you to
release it into your world and live your dreams.
Today, bring your dreams into your world!

MORNING REFLECTION: Date: _____

1. What is your reflection from today's quote?
   _____
   _____

2. Into which shoes do you need to step to move forward in this area of your life?
   _____
   _____

3. Out of which shoes do you need to step that hold you back?
   _____
   _____

4. What is the one step you can take today to move forward?
   _____
   _____

5. Your life resolution for today:
   "I commit to (action) _____ today, as I
   move closer to experiencing _____ in my life!"

6. With whom will you share today's life resolution to help hold you accountable?
   _____

EVENING REFLECTION:

Which insights will you take into tomorrow?
_____
_____

Day 62

Stand before the light of the universe and let it guide your next steps. Today, have no fear, simply trust in all that is within, around, and before you.

MORNING REFLECTION: Date: _____

1. What is your reflection from today's quote?
   _____
   _____

2. Into which shoes do you need to step to move forward in this area of your life?
   _____
   _____

3. Out of which shoes do you need to step that hold you back?
   _____
   _____

4. What is the one step you can take today to move forward?
   _____
   _____

5. Your life resolution for today:
   "I commit to (action) _____ today, as I move closer to experiencing _____ in my life!"

6. With whom will you share today's life resolution to help hold you accountable?
   _____

EVENING REFLECTION:

Which insights will you take into tomorrow?
_____
_____

Day 63

With your inner light, you can light up your life
and the world around. Today, shine bright!

MORNING REFLECTION: Date: _____

1. What is your reflection from today's quote?
   _____
   _____

2. Into which shoes do you need to step to move forward in this area of your life?
   _____
   _____

3. Out of which shoes do you need to step that hold you back?
   _____
   _____

4. What is the one step you can take today to move forward?
   _____
   _____

5. Your life resolution for today:
   "I commit to (action) _____ today, as I
   move closer to experiencing _____ in my life!"

6. With whom will you share today's life resolution to help hold you accountable?
   _____

EVENING REFLECTION:

Which insights will you take into tomorrow?
_____
_____

Day 64

If you ever start to think that you are "only" a small part of the universe, change your thinking to see that you are an extension of the grandest canyons and most infinite horizons. Today, sit in the grandeur of your infinite being!

## MORNING REFLECTION: 	Date: _____

1. What is your reflection from today's quote?

2. Into which shoes do you need to step to move forward in this area of your life?

3. Out of which shoes do you need to step that hold you back?

4. What is the one step you can take today to move forward?

5. Your life resolution for today:
   "I commit to (action) _____ today, as I move closer to experiencing _____ in my life!"

6. With whom will you share today's life resolution to help hold you accountable?

EVENING REFLECTION:

Which insights will you take into tomorrow?

Day 65

Take notice when you feel your life is moving too fast.
Today, give yourself permission to slow down.

MORNING REFLECTION: Date:

1. What is your reflection from today's quote?

2. Into which shoes do you need to step to move forward in this area of your life?

3. Out of which shoes do you need to step that hold you back?

4. What is the one step you can take today to move forward?

5. Your life resolution for today:
   "I commit to (action) _____ today, as I move closer to experiencing _____ in my life!"

6. With whom will you share today's life resolution to help hold you accountable?

EVENING REFLECTION:

Which insights will you take into tomorrow?

Day 66

You can write the pages of your life and fill them with magic that takes you on wondrous journeys. Today, be magical!

MORNING REFLECTION: Date: _____

1. What is your reflection from today's quote?
   _____
   _____

2. Into which shoes do you need to step to move forward in this area of your life?
   _____
   _____

3. Out of which shoes do you need to step that hold you back?
   _____
   _____

4. What is the one step you can take today to move forward?
   _____
   _____

5. Your life resolution for today:
   "I commit to (action) _____ today, as I move closer to experiencing _____ in my life!"

6. With whom will you share today's life resolution to help hold you accountable?
   _____

EVENING REFLECTION:

Which insights will you take into tomorrow?
   _____

Day 67

There is no need to restrain yourself in your life. You were born into unlimited possibilities. Today, identify just one step you can take into your possibilities, and take it!

MORNING REFLECTION: Date: _____

1. What is your reflection from today's quote?

2. Into which shoes do you need to step to move forward in this area of your life?

3. Out of which shoes do you need to step that hold you back?

4. What is the one step you can take today to move forward?

5. Your life resolution for today:
   "I commit to (action) _____ today, as I move closer to experiencing _____ in my life!"

6. With whom will you share today's life resolution to help hold you accountable?

EVENING REFLECTION:

Which insights will you take into tomorrow?

Day 68

Today, allow yourself to be born again. Thrive in the new life you choose to create!

MORNING REFLECTION: Date: _____

1. What is your reflection from today's quote?
   _____
   _____

2. Into which shoes do you need to step to move forward in this area of your life?
   _____
   _____

3. Out of which shoes do you need to step that hold you back?
   _____
   _____

4. What is the one step you can take today to move forward?
   _____
   _____

5. Your life resolution for today:
   "I commit to (action) _____ today, as I move closer to experiencing _____ in my life!"

6. With whom will you share today's life resolution to help hold you accountable?
   _____

EVENING REFLECTION:

Which insights will you take into tomorrow?
_____
_____

Day 69

The love that can bind each of us is present in every moment. It is our choice to embrace each other in love, or look for reasons to not. Today, look for reasons to love.

MORNING REFLECTION: Date: _____

1. What is your reflection from today's quote?
   _____
   _____

2. Into which shoes do you need to step to move forward in this area of your life?
   _____
   _____

3. Out of which shoes do you need to step that hold you back?
   _____
   _____

4. What is the one step you can take today to move forward?
   _____
   _____

5. Your life resolution for today:
   "I commit to (action) _____ today, as I move closer to experiencing _____ in my life!"

6. With whom will you share today's life resolution to help hold you accountable?
   _____

EVENING REFLECTION:

Which insights will you take into tomorrow?
_____

Day 70

We each have within us an angel, waiting to be released into our world. Today, let your angel fly, and allow yourself to be taken!

MORNING REFLECTION: Date: _____

1. What is your reflection from today's quote?
   _____
   _____

2. Into which shoes do you need to step to move forward in this area of your life?
   _____
   _____

3. Out of which shoes do you need to step that hold you back?
   _____
   _____

4. What is the one step you can take today to move forward?
   _____
   _____

5. Your life resolution for today:
   "I commit to (action) _____ today, as I
   move closer to experiencing _____ in my life!"

6. With whom will you share today's life resolution to help hold you accountable?
   _____

EVENING REFLECTION:

Which insights will you take into tomorrow?
_____
_____

Day 71

Today. Be happy. Be you. Be.

MORNING REFLECTION: Date: _____

1. What is your reflection from today's quote?
   _____
   _____

2. Into which shoes do you need to step to move forward in this area of your life?
   _____
   _____

3. Out of which shoes do you need to step that hold you back?
   _____
   _____

4. What is the one step you can take today to move forward?
   _____
   _____

5. Your life resolution for today:
   "I commit to (action) _____ today, as I
   move closer to experiencing _____ in my life!"

6. With whom will you share today's life resolution to help hold you accountable?
   _____

EVENING REFLECTION:

Which insights will you take into tomorrow?
_____
_____

Day 72

Once we feel the compass within us, we find new paths and new ways of being that are of our own creation. Today, allow your compass to guide you to paths that free you!

MORNING REFLECTION: Date: _____

1. What is your reflection from today's quote?
   _____
   _____

2. Into which shoes do you need to step to move forward in this area of your life?
   _____
   _____

3. Out of which shoes do you need to step that hold you back?
   _____
   _____

4. What is the one step you can take today to move forward?
   _____
   _____

5. Your life resolution for today:
   "I commit to (action) _____ today, as I move closer to experiencing _____ in my life!"

6. With whom will you share today's life resolution to help hold you accountable?
   _____

EVENING REFLECTION:

Which insights will you take into tomorrow?
_____
_____

Day 73

As children, we fill ourselves with wonder, color, magic, excitement, and adventure as we look into the world around. Today, let your child within show the adult the wonder in your world!

MORNING REFLECTION: Date: _____

1. What is your reflection from today's quote?
   _____
   _____

2. Into which shoes do you need to step to move forward in this area of your life?
   _____
   _____

3. Out of which shoes do you need to step that hold you back?
   _____
   _____

4. What is the one step you can take today to move forward?
   _____
   _____

5. Your life resolution for today:
   "I commit to (action) _____ today, as I move closer to experiencing _____ in my life!"

6. With whom will you share today's life resolution to help hold you accountable?
   _____

EVENING REFLECTION:

Which insights will you take into tomorrow?
_____
_____

Day 74

You must commit to take care of you. Without your best you, you cannot be your best. Today, commit one act of love toward you!

MORNING REFLECTION: Date: _____

1. What is your reflection from today's quote?
   _____
   _____

2. Into which shoes do you need to step to move forward in this area of your life?
   _____

3. Out of which shoes do you need to step that hold you back?
   _____

4. What is the one step you can take today to move forward?
   _____

5. Your life resolution for today:
   "I commit to (action) _____ today, as I move closer to experiencing _____ in my life!"

6. With whom will you share today's life resolution to help hold you accountable?
   _____

EVENING REFLECTION:

Which insights will you take into tomorrow?
_____
_____

Day 75

You only fail when you think so.
Today, think differently!

MORNING REFLECTION: Date: _____

1. What is your reflection from today's quote?
   _____
   _____

2. Into which shoes do you need to step to move forward in this area of your life?
   _____
   _____

3. Out of which shoes do you need to step that hold you back?
   _____
   _____

4. What is the one step you can take today to move forward?
   _____
   _____

5. Your life resolution for today:
   "I commit to (action) _____ today, as I
   move closer to experiencing _____ in my life!"

6. With whom will you share today's life resolution to help hold you accountable?
   _____

EVENING REFLECTION:

Which insights will you take into tomorrow?
_____
_____

Day 76

We are often our harshest critic. Today, be kind to yourself. Accept yourself. Forgive yourself. Love yourself.

MORNING REFLECTION: Date: _____

1. What is your reflection from today's quote?
   _____

2. Into which shoes do you need to step to move forward in this area of your life?
   _____

3. Out of which shoes do you need to step that hold you back?
   _____

4. What is the one step you can take today to move forward?
   _____

5. Your life resolution for today:
   "I commit to (action) _____ today, as I move closer to experiencing _____ in my life!"

6. With whom will you share today's life resolution to help hold you accountable?
   _____

EVENING REFLECTION:

Which insights will you take into tomorrow?
_____

Day 77

As children, play brought us to life. As adults, play rejuvenates the child within us. Today, play!

MORNING REFLECTION: Date:

1. What is your reflection from today's quote?

2. Into which shoes do you need to step to move forward in this area of your life?

3. Out of which shoes do you need to step that hold you back?

4. What is the one step you can take today to move forward?

5. Your life resolution for today:
   "I commit to (action) _____ today, as I move closer to experiencing _____ in my life!"

6. With whom will you share today's life resolution to help hold you accountable?

EVENING REFLECTION:

Which insights will you take into tomorrow?

Day 78

When we stop to smell the flowers, we find gardens surrounding us. Today, stop and smell the flowers and allow your gardens to emerge.

MORNING REFLECTION: Date: _____

1. What is your reflection from today's quote?
   _____
   _____

2. Into which shoes do you need to step to move forward in this area of your life?
   _____
   _____

3. Out of which shoes do you need to step that hold you back?
   _____
   _____

4. What is the one step you can take today to move forward?
   _____
   _____

5. Your life resolution for today:
   "I commit to (action) _____ today, as I move closer to experiencing _____ in my life!"

6. With whom will you share today's life resolution to help hold you accountable?

EVENING REFLECTION:

Which insights will you take into tomorrow?
_____
_____

Day 79

As you conquer those parts of your "self" that don't serve you, you create more space for pieces of your "self" that are born of your soul to emerge. Today, conquer your "self" and create space for your soul to emerge!

MORNING REFLECTION: Date: _____

1. What is your reflection from today's quote?

2. Into which shoes do you need to step to move forward in this area of your life?

3. Out of which shoes do you need to step that hold you back?

4. What is the one step you can take today to move forward?

5. Your life resolution for today:
   "I commit to (action) _____ today, as I move closer to experiencing _____ in my life!"

6. With whom will you share today's life resolution to help hold you accountable?

EVENING REFLECTION:

Which insights will you take into tomorrow?

Day 80

You are your greatest gift.
Today, open yourself and burst into the world!

MORNING REFLECTION: Date: _____

1. What is your reflection from today's quote?
   _____
   _____

2. Into which shoes do you need to step to move forward in this area of your life?
   _____
   _____

3. Out of which shoes do you need to step that hold you back?
   _____
   _____

4. What is the one step you can take today to move forward?
   _____
   _____

5. Your life resolution for today:
   "I commit to (action) _____ today, as I
   move closer to experiencing _____ in my life!"

6. With whom will you share today's life resolution to help hold you accountable?
   _____

EVENING REFLECTION:

Which insights will you take into tomorrow?
_____
_____

Day 81

Love begins at home. Today, love you!

MORNING REFLECTION: Date: _____

1. What is your reflection from today's quote?
   _____
   _____

2. Into which shoes do you need to step to move forward in this area of your life?
   _____
   _____

3. Out of which shoes do you need to step that hold you back?
   _____
   _____

4. What is the one step you can take today to move forward?
   _____
   _____

5. Your life resolution for today:
   "I commit to (action) _____ today, as I move closer to experiencing _____ in my life!"

6. With whom will you share today's life resolution to help hold you accountable?
   _____

EVENING REFLECTION:

Which insights will you take into tomorrow?
_____
_____

Day 82

A beautiful garden lies within you.
Today, let it blossom and emerge to color your world.

MORNING REFLECTION: Date: _____

1. What is your reflection from today's quote?

2. Into which shoes do you need to step to move forward in this area of your life?

3. Out of which shoes do you need to step that hold you back?

4. What is the one step you can take today to move forward?

5. Your life resolution for today:
   "I commit to (action) _____ today, as I move closer to experiencing _____ in my life!"

6. With whom will you share today's life resolution to help hold you accountable?

EVENING REFLECTION:

Which insights will you take into tomorrow?

Day 83

The present is filled with gifts, waiting for us to pause and
see them. Today, lose a minute and find your gifts!

MORNING REFLECTION: Date: _____

1. What is your reflection from today's quote?
   _____
   _____

2. Into which shoes do you need to step to move forward in this area of your life?
   _____
   _____

3. Out of which shoes do you need to step that hold you back?
   _____
   _____

4. What is the one step you can take today to move forward?
   _____
   _____

5. Your life resolution for today:
   "I commit to (action) _____ today, as I
   move closer to experiencing _____ in my life!"

6. With whom will you share today's life resolution to help hold you accountable?
   _____

EVENING REFLECTION:

Which insights will you take into tomorrow?
_____
_____

Day 84

Each day as we wake, we have the opportunity to step into the life of our dreams. Today, take a step into your dreams!

MORNING REFLECTION: Date: _____

1. What is your reflection from today's quote?
   _____

2. Into which shoes do you need to step to move forward in this area of your life?
   _____

3. Out of which shoes do you need to step that hold you back?
   _____

4. What is the one step you can take today to move forward?
   _____

5. Your life resolution for today:
   "I commit to (action) _____ today, as I move closer to experiencing _____ in my life!"

6. With whom will you share today's life resolution to help hold you accountable?
   _____

EVENING REFLECTION:

Which insights will you take into tomorrow?
_____

Day 85

Our greatness is present within us every day.
Today, unwrap it!

MORNING REFLECTION: Date: _____

1. What is your reflection from today's quote?

2. Into which shoes do you need to step to move forward in this area of your life?

3. Out of which shoes do you need to step that hold you back?

4. What is the one step you can take today to move forward?

5. Your life resolution for today:
   "I commit to (action) _____ today, as I move closer to experiencing _____ in my life!"

6. With whom will you share today's life resolution to help hold you accountable?

EVENING REFLECTION:

Which insights will you take into tomorrow?

Day 86

Your dreams are like magical auras, waiting to burst into brilliant color and light as they move with you through each moment. Today, bring your auras to life!

MORNING REFLECTION: Date: _____

1. What is your reflection from today's quote?
   _____
   _____

2. Into which shoes do you need to step to move forward in this area of your life?
   _____
   _____

3. Out of which shoes do you need to step that hold you back?
   _____
   _____

4. What is the one step you can take today to move forward?
   _____
   _____

5. Your life resolution for today:
   "I commit to (action) _____ today, as I move closer to experiencing _____ in my life!"

6. With whom will you share today's life resolution to help hold you accountable?
   _____

EVENING REFLECTION:

Which insights will you take into tomorrow?
_____
_____

Day 87

Decide what you want. Today, take action.

MORNING REFLECTION: Date: _____

1. What is your reflection from today's quote?
   _____
   _____

2. Into which shoes do you need to step to move forward in this area of your life?
   _____
   _____

3. Out of which shoes do you need to step that hold you back?
   _____
   _____

4. What is the one step you can take today to move forward?
   _____
   _____

5. Your life resolution for today:
   "I commit to (action) _____ today, as I move closer to experiencing _____ in my life!"

6. With whom will you share today's life resolution to help hold you accountable?
   _____

EVENING REFLECTION:

Which insights will you take into tomorrow?
_____
_____

Day 88

You have the choice to act for yourself every day. Today, act for you.

MORNING REFLECTION: Date: _____

1. What is your reflection from today's quote?
   _____
   _____

2. Into which shoes do you need to step to move forward in this area of your life?
   _____
   _____

3. Out of which shoes do you need to step that hold you back?
   _____
   _____

4. What is the one step you can take today to move forward?
   _____
   _____

5. Your life resolution for today:
   "I commit to (action) _____ today, as I move closer to experiencing _____ in my life!"

6. With whom will you share today's life resolution to help hold you accountable?
   _____

EVENING REFLECTION:

Which insights will you take into tomorrow?
_____
_____

Day 89

The more we feed ourselves with simple acts of kindness,
the more we grow the seeds of our limitless potential that
are within us. Today, feed yourself with kindness.

MORNING REFLECTION: Date: _____

1. What is your reflection from today's quote?
   _____
   _____

2. Into which shoes do you need to step to move forward in this area of your life?
   _____
   _____

3. Out of which shoes do you need to step that hold you back?
   _____
   _____

4. What is the one step you can take today to move forward?
   _____
   _____

5. Your life resolution for today:
   "I commit to (action) _____ today, as I
   move closer to experiencing _____ in my life!"

6. With whom will you share today's life resolution to help hold you accountable?
   _____

EVENING REFLECTION:

Which insights will you take into tomorrow?
_____
_____

Day 90

Each morning, the sun rises and sheds light on your life. Today, see the light.

MORNING REFLECTION: Date: _____

1. What is your reflection from today's quote?
   _____
   _____

2. Into which shoes do you need to step to move forward in this area of your life?
   _____
   _____

3. Out of which shoes do you need to step that hold you back?
   _____
   _____

4. What is the one step you can take today to move forward?
   _____
   _____

5. Your life resolution for today:
   "I commit to (action) _____ today, as I move closer to experiencing _____ in my life!"

6. With whom will you share today's life resolution to help hold you accountable?
   _____

EVENING REFLECTION:

Which insights will you take into tomorrow?
_____
_____

Day 91

We are not alone in our pain, yet so often we enable our pain to create walls that separate and divide us, rather than allow it to bring us together. Today, allow your pain to be a bridge to another.

MORNING REFLECTION:

Date: _____

1. What is your reflection from today's quote?

2. Into which shoes do you need to step to move forward in this area of your life?

3. Out of which shoes do you need to step that hold you back?

4. What is the one step you can take today to move forward?

5. Your life resolution for today:
   "I commit to (action) _____ today, as I move closer to experiencing _____ in my life!"

6. With whom will you share today's life resolution to help hold you accountable?

EVENING REFLECTION:

Which insights will you take into tomorrow?

Day 92

Each day we awaken to continue to paint the picture of our lives. Today, allow your passion to burst into color on your canvas!

MORNING REFLECTION: Date: _____

1. What is your reflection from today's quote?
   _____
   _____

2. Into which shoes do you need to step to move forward in this area of your life?
   _____
   _____

3. Out of which shoes do you need to step that hold you back?
   _____
   _____

4. What is the one step you can take today to move forward?
   _____
   _____

5. Your life resolution for today:
   "I commit to (action) _____ today, as I move closer to experiencing _____ in my life!"

6. With whom will you share today's life resolution to help hold you accountable?
   _____

EVENING REFLECTION:

Which insights will you take into tomorrow?
_____
_____

Day 93

Our lives can be consumed by tasks, or moved by moments.
Today, allow yourself to be moved by moments.

MORNING REFLECTION: Date:

1. What is your reflection from today's quote?

2. Into which shoes do you need to step to move forward in this area of your life?

3. Out of which shoes do you need to step that hold you back?

4. What is the one step you can take today to move forward?

5. Your life resolution for today:
   "I commit to (action) _____ today, as I move closer to experiencing _____ in my life!"

6. With whom will you share today's life resolution to help hold you accountable?

EVENING REFLECTION:

Which insights will you take into tomorrow?

Day 94
Be love. Today, allow love.

MORNING REFLECTION: Date: _____

1. What is your reflection from today's quote?
   _____
   _____

2. Into which shoes do you need to step to move forward in this area of your life?
   _____
   _____

3. Out of which shoes do you need to step that hold you back?
   _____
   _____

4. What is the one step you can take today to move forward?
   _____
   _____

5. Your life resolution for today:
   "I commit to (action) _____ today, as I
   move closer to experiencing _____ in my life!"

6. With whom will you share today's life resolution to help hold you accountable?
   _____

EVENING REFLECTION:
Which insights will you take into tomorrow?
_____
_____

Day 95

We are all part of evolution. Today, evolve!

MORNING REFLECTION: Date: _____

1. What is your reflection from today's quote?
   _____
   _____

2. Into which shoes do you need to step to move forward in this area of your life?
   _____
   _____

3. Out of which shoes do you need to step that hold you back?
   _____
   _____

4. What is the one step you can take today to move forward?
   _____
   _____

5. Your life resolution for today:
   "I commit to (action) _____ today, as I move closer to experiencing _____ in my life!"

6. With whom will you share today's life resolution to help hold you accountable?
   _____

EVENING REFLECTION:

Which insights will you take into tomorrow?
_____

Day 96

Our imaginations enable us to envision our greatest lives.
Our being brings our imagination into reality.
Today, be all you imagine!

MORNING REFLECTION: Date:

1. What is your reflection from today's quote?

2. Into which shoes do you need to step to move forward in this area of your life?

3. Out of which shoes do you need to step that hold you back?

4. What is the one step you can take today to move forward?

5. Your life resolution for today:
   "I commit to (action) _____ today, as I move closer to experiencing _____ in my life!"

6. With whom will you share today's life resolution to help hold you accountable?

EVENING REFLECTION:

Which insights will you take into tomorrow?

Day 97

Are you doing enough of "less" to "be" more?
Today, pause and be more.

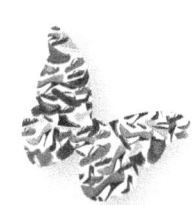

MORNING REFLECTION: Date:

1. What is your reflection from today's quote?

2. Into which shoes do you need to step to move forward in this area of your life?

3. Out of which shoes do you need to step that hold you back?

4. What is the one step you can take today to move forward?

5. Your life resolution for today:
   "I commit to (action) _____ today, as I move closer to experiencing _____ in my life!"

6. With whom will you share today's life resolution to help hold you accountable?

EVENING REFLECTION:

Which insights will you take into tomorrow?

Day 98

The life force that flows through us enables us to live, to laugh, and to love. It is our fuel of life. Today, fuel yourself with your life force.

MORNING REFLECTION: Date: _____

1. What is your reflection from today's quote?
   _____
   _____

2. Into which shoes do you need to step to move forward in this area of your life?
   _____
   _____

3. Out of which shoes do you need to step that hold you back?
   _____
   _____

4. What is the one step you can take today to move forward?
   _____
   _____

5. Your life resolution for today:
   "I commit to (action) _____ today, as I move closer to experiencing _____ in my life!"

6. With whom will you share today's life resolution to help hold you accountable?
   _____

EVENING REFLECTION:

Which insights will you take into tomorrow?
_____
_____

Day 99

As children, the world around fills us with awe. As adults, our worlds within allow us to create awe around us. Today, be awesome!

MORNING REFLECTION: Date: _____

1. What is your reflection from today's quote?

2. Into which shoes do you need to step to move forward in this area of your life?

3. Out of which shoes do you need to step that hold you back?

4. What is the one step you can take today to move forward?

5. Your life resolution for today:
   "I commit to (action) _____ today, as I move closer to experiencing _____ in my life!"

6. With whom will you share today's life resolution to help hold you accountable?

EVENING REFLECTION:

Which insights will you take into tomorrow?

Day 100
You already "are." All you need to do is "be." Today, be.

MORNING REFLECTION: Date:

1. What is your reflection from today's quote?

2. Into which shoes do you need to step to move forward in this area of your life?

3. Out of which shoes do you need to step that hold you back?

4. What is the one step you can take today to move forward?

5. Your life resolution for today:
   "I commit to (action) _____ today, as I move closer to experiencing _____ in my life!"

6. With whom will you share today's life resolution to help hold you accountable?

EVENING REFLECTION:

Which insights will you take into tomorrow?

Day 101

We each have wings waiting for us to lift them. Today, fly!

MORNING REFLECTION: Date: _____

1. What is your reflection from today's quote?
   _____
   _____

2. Into which shoes do you need to step to move forward in this area of your life?
   _____
   _____

3. Out of which shoes do you need to step that hold you back?
   _____
   _____

4. What is the one step you can take today to move forward?
   _____
   _____

5. Your life resolution for today:
   "I commit to (action) _____ today, as I move closer to experiencing _____ in my life!"

6. With whom will you share today's life resolution to help hold you accountable?
   _____

EVENING REFLECTION:

Which insights will you take into tomorrow?
_____
_____

Day 102

Call "it" God, your higher power, your source, your soul.
Today, let "it" guide you!

MORNING REFLECTION: Date: _____

1. What is your reflection from today's quote?

2. Into which shoes do you need to step to move forward in this area of your life?

3. Out of which shoes do you need to step that hold you back?

4. What is the one step you can take today to move forward?

5. Your life resolution for today:
   "I commit to (action) _____ today, as I move closer to experiencing _____ in my life!"

6. With whom will you share today's life resolution to help hold you accountable?

EVENING REFLECTION:

Which insights will you take into tomorrow?

Day 103

You are your greatest expression of unconditional love.
Today, express yourself ... unconditionally!

MORNING REFLECTION: Date: _____

1. What is your reflection from today's quote?
   _____
   _____

2. Into which shoes do you need to step to move forward in this area of your life?
   _____
   _____

3. Out of which shoes do you need to step that hold you back?
   _____
   _____

4. What is the one step you can take today to move forward?
   _____
   _____

5. Your life resolution for today:
   "I commit to (action) _____ today, as I move closer to experiencing _____ in my life!"

6. With whom will you share today's life resolution to help hold you accountable?
   _____

EVENING REFLECTION:

Which insights will you take into tomorrow?
_____
_____

Day 104

In the world, there are leaders, followers, and those who sit on the fence. Those who dare to be leaders will change the world. Today, lead!

MORNING REFLECTION: Date: _____

1. What is your reflection from today's quote?
   _____
   _____

2. Into which shoes do you need to step to move forward in this area of your life?
   _____
   _____

3. Out of which shoes do you need to step that hold you back?
   _____
   _____

4. What is the one step you can take today to move forward?
   _____
   _____

5. Your life resolution for today:
   "I commit to (action) _____ today, as I move closer to experiencing _____ in my life!"

6. With whom will you share today's life resolution to help hold you accountable?
   _____

EVENING REFLECTION:

Which insights will you take into tomorrow?
_____
_____

Day 105

When we strip everything away, we are one. One infinite consciousness. One infinite source. Infinitely bound to each other. Today, be "one."

MORNING REFLECTION: Date: _____

1. What is your reflection from today's quote?
   _____
   _____

2. Into which shoes do you need to step to move forward in this area of your life?
   _____
   _____

3. Out of which shoes do you need to step that hold you back?
   _____
   _____

4. What is the one step you can take today to move forward?
   _____
   _____

5. Your life resolution for today:
   "I commit to (action) _____ today, as I move closer to experiencing _____ in my life!"

6. With whom will you share today's life resolution to help hold you accountable?
   _____

EVENING REFLECTION:

Which insights will you take into tomorrow?
_____
_____

Day 106

"Be" your greatest. Today, leap into your being!

MORNING REFLECTION: Date: _____

1. What is your reflection from today's quote?

2. Into which shoes do you need to step to move forward in this area of your life?

3. Out of which shoes do you need to step that hold you back?

4. What is the one step you can take today to move forward?

5. Your life resolution for today:
   "I commit to (action) _____ today, as I move closer to experiencing _____ in my life!"

6. With whom will you share today's life resolution to help hold you accountable?

EVENING REFLECTION:

Which insights will you take into tomorrow?

Day 107

The power to change is in our hands, arising in each moment,
waiting for us to be lifted in its wings. Today, be lifted!

MORNING REFLECTION: Date: _____

1. What is your reflection from today's quote?
   _____
   _____

2. Into which shoes do you need to step to move forward in this area of your life?
   _____
   _____

3. Out of which shoes do you need to step that hold you back?
   _____
   _____

4. What is the one step you can take today to move forward?
   _____
   _____

5. Your life resolution for today:
   "I commit to (action) _____ today, as I
   move closer to experiencing _____ in my life!"

6. With whom will you share today's life resolution to help hold you accountable?
   _____

EVENING REFLECTION:

Which insights will you take into tomorrow?
_____
_____

Day 108

As sentient beings, we have the ability to affect change, or accept circumstance. It is our choice in each moment. Today, pause and affect!

MORNING REFLECTION: Date: _____

1. What is your reflection from today's quote?
   _____
   _____

2. Into which shoes do you need to step to move forward in this area of your life?
   _____
   _____

3. Out of which shoes do you need to step that hold you back?
   _____
   _____

4. What is the one step you can take today to move forward?
   _____
   _____

5. Your life resolution for today:
   "I commit to (action) _____ today, as I move closer to experiencing _____ in my life!"

6. With whom will you share today's life resolution to help hold you accountable?
   _____

EVENING REFLECTION:

Which insights will you take into tomorrow?
_____
_____

Day 109

Your life is your greatest treasure.
Today, leap into your fortune!

MORNING REFLECTION: Date: _____

1. What is your reflection from today's quote?
   _____
   _____

2. Into which shoes do you need to step to move forward in this area of your life?
   _____
   _____

3. Out of which shoes do you need to step that hold you back?
   _____
   _____

4. What is the one step you can take today to move forward?
   _____
   _____

5. Your life resolution for today:
   "I commit to (action) _____ today, as I move closer to experiencing _____ in my life!"

6. With whom will you share today's life resolution to help hold you accountable?
   _____

EVENING REFLECTION:

Which insights will you take into tomorrow?
   _____
   _____

Day 110

With our eyes we see anew all that is around us.
Today, see anew all that is within you!

MORNING REFLECTION: Date: _____

1. What is your reflection from today's quote?

2. Into which shoes do you need to step to move forward in this area of your life?

3. Out of which shoes do you need to step that hold you back?

4. What is the one step you can take today to move forward?

5. Your life resolution for today:
   "I commit to (action) _____ today, as I move closer to experiencing _____ in my life!"

6. With whom will you share today's life resolution to help hold you accountable?

EVENING REFLECTION:

Which insights will you take into tomorrow?

Day 111

You can use every moment to uncover the pieces of your greatest self, to discover the treasures that lie within, and to reveal the life that is born of your soul. Today, uncover, discover, reveal!

MORNING REFLECTION: Date: _____

1. What is your reflection from today's quote?
   _____
   _____

2. Into which shoes do you need to step to move forward in this area of your life?
   _____
   _____

3. Out of which shoes do you need to step that hold you back?
   _____
   _____

4. What is the one step you can take today to move forward?
   _____
   _____

5. Your life resolution for today:
   "I commit to (action) _____ today, as I move closer to experiencing _____ in my life!"

6. With whom will you share today's life resolution to help hold you accountable?
   _____

EVENING REFLECTION:

Which insights will you take into tomorrow?
   _____

Day 112

With our thoughts, we create our world.
Today, take care of your thoughts.

MORNING REFLECTION: Date: _____

1. What is your reflection from today's quote?
   _____

2. Into which shoes do you need to step to move forward in this area of your life?
   _____

3. Out of which shoes do you need to step that hold you back?
   _____

4. What is the one step you can take today to move forward?
   _____

5. Your life resolution for today:
   "I commit to (action) _____ today, as I move closer to experiencing _____ in my life!"

6. With whom will you share today's life resolution to help hold you accountable?
   _____

EVENING REFLECTION:

Which insights will you take into tomorrow?
_____

Day 113

What you believe, takes over you.
Today, believe in the extraordinary!

MORNING REFLECTION: Date: _____

1. What is your reflection from today's quote?
   _____
   _____

2. Into which shoes do you need to step to move forward in this area of your life?
   _____
   _____

3. Out of which shoes do you need to step that hold you back?
   _____
   _____

4. What is the one step you can take today to move forward?
   _____
   _____

5. Your life resolution for today:
   "I commit to (action) _____ today, as I move closer to experiencing _____ in my life!"

6. With whom will you share today's life resolution to help hold you accountable?
   _____

EVENING REFLECTION:

Which insights will you take into tomorrow?
_____
_____

Day 114

You are your greatest truth.
Today, look within for the answers you need.

MORNING REFLECTION: Date: _____

1. What is your reflection from today's quote?

2. Into which shoes do you need to step to move forward in this area of your life?

3. Out of which shoes do you need to step that hold you back?

4. What is the one step you can take today to move forward?

5. Your life resolution for today:
   "I commit to (action) _____ today, as I move closer to experiencing _____ in my life!"

6. With whom will you share today's life resolution to help hold you accountable?

EVENING REFLECTION:

Which insights will you take into tomorrow?

Day 115

Within us is the force that can transform the world around us. Today, transform your world!

MORNING REFLECTION: Date: _____

1. What is your reflection from today's quote?
   _____
   _____

2. Into which shoes do you need to step to move forward in this area of your life?
   _____
   _____

3. Out of which shoes do you need to step that hold you back?
   _____
   _____

4. What is the one step you can take today to move forward?
   _____
   _____

5. Your life resolution for today:
   "I commit to (action) _____ today, as I move closer to experiencing _____ in my life!"

6. With whom will you share today's life resolution to help hold you accountable?
   _____

EVENING REFLECTION:

Which insights will you take into tomorrow?
_____
_____

Day 116

Step out of the busyness around you,
and into the powerful serenity within you.
It is only a pause away. Today, pause.

MORNING REFLECTION: Date: _____

1. What is your reflection from today's quote?
   _____
   _____

2. Into which shoes do you need to step to move forward in this area of your life?
   _____
   _____

3. Out of which shoes do you need to step that hold you back?
   _____
   _____

4. What is the one step you can take today to move forward?
   _____
   _____

5. Your life resolution for today:
   "I commit to (action) _____ today, as I
   move closer to experiencing _____ in my life!"

6. With whom will you share today's life resolution to help hold you accountable?
   _____

EVENING REFLECTION:

Which insights will you take into tomorrow?
_____

Day 117

One must step bravely into the heights and just as bravely into the depths. Then we will find the truths that light our way. Today, let your truths light your way.

MORNING REFLECTION: Date: _____

1. What is your reflection from today's quote?
   _____
   _____

2. Into which shoes do you need to step to move forward in this area of your life?
   _____
   _____

3. Out of which shoes do you need to step that hold you back?
   _____
   _____

4. What is the one step you can take today to move forward?
   _____
   _____

5. Your life resolution for today:
   "I commit to (action) _____ today, as I move closer to experiencing _____ in my life!"

6. With whom will you share today's life resolution to help hold you accountable?
   _____

EVENING REFLECTION:

Which insights will you take into tomorrow?
_____
_____

Day 118

Fall in love with yourself, fall in love with life, then fall in love with another. Today, fall in love!

MORNING REFLECTION: Date: _____

1. What is your reflection from today's quote?
   _____
   _____

2. Into which shoes do you need to step to move forward in this area of your life?
   _____
   _____

3. Out of which shoes do you need to step that hold you back?
   _____
   _____

4. What is the one step you can take today to move forward?
   _____
   _____

5. Your life resolution for today:
   "I commit to (action) _____ today, as I move closer to experiencing _____ in my life!"

6. With whom will you share today's life resolution to help hold you accountable?
   _____

EVENING REFLECTION:

Which insights will you take into tomorrow?
_____
_____

Day 119

What do we see of the world that stands before us—steps upon which we can climb to discover magic and mystery, or obstacles that cause us to remain stuck in the same shoes, in the same place? Today, step into your discovery shoes!

MORNING REFLECTION: Date: _____

1. What is your reflection from today's quote?
   _____
   _____

2. Into which shoes do you need to step to move forward in this area of your life?
   _____
   _____

3. Out of which shoes do you need to step that hold you back?
   _____
   _____

4. What is the one step you can take today to move forward?
   _____
   _____

5. Your life resolution for today:
   "I commit to (action) _____ today, as I move closer to experiencing _____ in my life!"

6. With whom will you share today's life resolution to help hold you accountable?
   _____

EVENING REFLECTION:

Which insights will you take into tomorrow?
_____
_____

Day 120

Unless we free ourselves from our pain, we are slaves to it. We can't rise above our pain if we are buried in it. Today, leave your pain behind, and leap into the extraordinary journey ahead of you!

MORNING REFLECTION: Date: _____

1. What is your reflection from today's quote?
   _____
   _____

2. Into which shoes do you need to step to move forward in this area of your life?
   _____
   _____

3. Out of which shoes do you need to step that hold you back?
   _____
   _____

4. What is the one step you can take today to move forward?
   _____
   _____

5. Your life resolution for today:
   "I commit to (action) _____ today, as I move closer to experiencing _____ in my life!"

6. With whom will you share today's life resolution to help hold you accountable?
   _____

EVENING REFLECTION:

Which insights will you take into tomorrow?
_____
_____

Day 121

In each day, we have the ability to come closer to ourselves, to tap into our soul, and to come to know, feel, and touch our inner being. Today, come close to you.

MORNING REFLECTION: Date: _____

1. What is your reflection from today's quote?

2. Into which shoes do you need to step to move forward in this area of your life?

3. Out of which shoes do you need to step that hold you back?

4. What is the one step you can take today to move forward?

5. Your life resolution for today:
   "I commit to (action) _____ today, as I move closer to experiencing _____ in my life!"

6. With whom will you share today's life resolution to help hold you accountable?

EVENING REFLECTION:

Which insights will you take into tomorrow?

Day 122

What can we accomplish in our lives if we are silent? How much impact can our lives have if we stay invisible and hidden away? Today, proclaim your life and make some noise!

MORNING REFLECTION: Date: _____

1. What is your reflection from today's quote?

2. Into which shoes do you need to step to move forward in this area of your life?

3. Out of which shoes do you need to step that hold you back?

4. What is the one step you can take today to move forward?

5. Your life resolution for today:
   "I commit to (action) _____ today, as I move closer to experiencing _____ in my life!"

6. With whom will you share today's life resolution to help hold you accountable?

EVENING REFLECTION:

Which insights will you take into tomorrow?

Day 123

The evidence of the greatness of our capabilities
is all around us—in its grandeur and in its detail.
Today, see the grandeur around and within you!

MORNING REFLECTION: Date: _____

1. What is your reflection from today's quote?
   _____
   _____

2. Into which shoes do you need to step to move forward in this area of your life?
   _____
   _____

3. Out of which shoes do you need to step that hold you back?
   _____
   _____

4. What is the one step you can take today to move forward?
   _____
   _____

5. Your life resolution for today:
   "I commit to (action) _____ today, as I
   move closer to experiencing _____ in my life!"

6. With whom will you share today's life resolution to help hold you accountable?
   _____

EVENING REFLECTION:

Which insights will you take into tomorrow?
_____
_____

Day 124

Be where you are, pause in the moment, see all that is within and around you. Today, live and love the present moment!

MORNING REFLECTION: Date: _____

1. What is your reflection from today's quote?

2. Into which shoes do you need to step to move forward in this area of your life?

3. Out of which shoes do you need to step that hold you back?

4. What is the one step you can take today to move forward?

5. Your life resolution for today:
   "I commit to (action) _____ today, as I move closer to experiencing _____ in my life!"

6. With whom will you share today's life resolution to help hold you accountable?

EVENING REFLECTION:

Which insights will you take into tomorrow?

Day 125

In each moment, we have awe all around us. We simply need to pause to experience it—look up to the sky, or out to the ocean, to the stars each night, or into the eyes of a friend. Today, pause to feel goosebumps of awe!

MORNING REFLECTION:　　　　　　　Date:

1. What is your reflection from today's quote?

2. Into which shoes do you need to step to move forward in this area of your life?

3. Out of which shoes do you need to step that hold you back?

4. What is the one step you can take today to move forward?

5. Your life resolution for today:
   "I commit to (action) _____ today, as I move closer to experiencing _____ in my life!"

6. With whom will you share today's life resolution to help hold you accountable?

EVENING REFLECTION:

Which insights will you take into tomorrow?

Day 126

How much energy do we consume day after day jumping from trend to trend, false hope to false hope, rather than pausing and being still to hear and feel our deepest and most authentic dreams and desires? Today, pause, feel your most meaningful desires!

MORNING REFLECTION: Date: _____

1. What is your reflection from today's quote?
   _____
   _____

2. Into which shoes do you need to step to move forward in this area of your life?
   _____
   _____

3. Out of which shoes do you need to step that hold you back?
   _____
   _____

4. What is the one step you can take today to move forward?
   _____
   _____

5. Your life resolution for today:
   "I commit to (action) _____ today, as I move closer to experiencing _____ in my life!"

6. With whom will you share today's life resolution to help hold you accountable?
   _____

EVENING REFLECTION:

Which insights will you take into tomorrow?
_____
_____

Day 127

Your home is within you—where, in that quiet space, you will find all that you seek—joy, serenity, confidence, purpose, strength, clarity, wisdom, compassion, love. Today, be at home!

MORNING REFLECTION: Date: _____

1. What is your reflection from today's quote?

2. Into which shoes do you need to step to move forward in this area of your life?

3. Out of which shoes do you need to step that hold you back?

4. What is the one step you can take today to move forward?

5. Your life resolution for today:
   "I commit to (action) _____ today, as I move closer to experiencing _____ in my life!"

6. With whom will you share today's life resolution to help hold you accountable?

EVENING REFLECTION:

Which insights will you take into tomorrow?

Day 128

You are your greatest treasure.
Today, unwrap yourself and shine!

MORNING REFLECTION: Date: _____

1. What is your reflection from today's quote?

2. Into which shoes do you need to step to move forward in this area of your life?

3. Out of which shoes do you need to step that hold you back?

4. What is the one step you can take today to move forward?

5. Your life resolution for today:
   "I commit to (action) _____ today, as I move closer to experiencing _____ in my life!"

6. With whom will you share today's life resolution to help hold you accountable?

EVENING REFLECTION:

Which insights will you take into tomorrow?

Day 129

All that is before you cannot be seen clearly until you pause to see it. Today, pause to bring into focus all the color and magic that is before you, and step purposefully forward into all you are here to be!

MORNING REFLECTION: Date: _____

1. What is your reflection from today's quote?
   _____
   _____

2. Into which shoes do you need to step to move forward in this area of your life?
   _____
   _____

3. Out of which shoes do you need to step that hold you back?
   _____
   _____

4. What is the one step you can take today to move forward?
   _____
   _____

5. Your life resolution for today:
   "I commit to (action) _____ today, as I move closer to experiencing _____ in my life!"

6. With whom will you share today's life resolution to help hold you accountable?
   _____

EVENING REFLECTION:

Which insights will you take into tomorrow?
_____
_____

Day 130

As you contemplate the life you desire, look within to reveal the "shoes" you need to leave behind, and those you need to take you forward with purpose and passion. Today, start to pack your new shoes!

MORNING REFLECTION: Date: _____

1. What is your reflection from today's quote?
   _____
   _____

2. Into which shoes do you need to step to move forward in this area of your life?
   _____
   _____

3. Out of which shoes do you need to step that hold you back?
   _____
   _____

4. What is the one step you can take today to move forward?
   _____
   _____

5. Your life resolution for today:
   "I commit to (action) _____ today, as I move closer to experiencing _____ in my life!"

6. With whom will you share today's life resolution to help hold you accountable?
   _____

EVENING REFLECTION:

Which insights will you take into tomorrow?
_____
_____

Day 131

As we step forward, we can choose to take only those things that strengthen and excite us. The rest can be left behind. Today, choose to release all that weakens and drains you!

MORNING REFLECTION: Date: _____

1. What is your reflection from today's quote?
   _____
   _____

2. Into which shoes do you need to step to move forward in this area of your life?
   _____
   _____

3. Out of which shoes do you need to step that hold you back?
   _____
   _____

4. What is the one step you can take today to move forward?
   _____
   _____

5. Your life resolution for today:
   "I commit to (action) _____ today, as I move closer to experiencing _____ in my life!"

6. With whom will you share today's life resolution to help hold you accountable?
   _____

EVENING REFLECTION:

Which insights will you take into tomorrow?
_____
_____

Day 132

With the richness of the colors of the sunrise, we can see the abundance within ourselves—bright, radiant, warm—touching each of us from one common source. Today, allow your abundance to shine on another.

MORNING REFLECTION: Date:

1. What is your reflection from today's quote?

2. Into which shoes do you need to step to move forward in this area of your life?

3. Out of which shoes do you need to step that hold you back?

4. What is the one step you can take today to move forward?

5. Your life resolution for today:
   "I commit to (action) _____ today, as I move closer to experiencing _____ in my life!"

6. With whom will you share today's life resolution to help hold you accountable?

EVENING REFLECTION:

Which insights will you take into tomorrow?

Day 133

With the dawn of every morning, there is new life. With each new morning, we can choose to rise into our future. Today, awaken, change your shoes, rise into your future!"

MORNING REFLECTION: Date: _____

1. What is your reflection from today's quote?
   _____
   _____

2. Into which shoes do you need to step to move forward in this area of your life?
   _____
   _____

3. Out of which shoes do you need to step that hold you back?
   _____
   _____

4. What is the one step you can take today to move forward?
   _____
   _____

5. Your life resolution for today:
   "I commit to (action) _____ today, as I move closer to experiencing _____ in my life!"

6. With whom will you share today's life resolution to help hold you accountable?
   _____

EVENING REFLECTION:

Which insights will you take into tomorrow?
_____
_____

Day 134

You are the sum of all your thoughts, words, and actions as you send them out into the world and touch those close to you and far from you. Today, touch another with love!

MORNING REFLECTION: Date: _____

1. What is your reflection from today's quote?
   _____
   _____

2. Into which shoes do you need to step to move forward in this area of your life?
   _____
   _____

3. Out of which shoes do you need to step that hold you back?
   _____
   _____

4. What is the one step you can take today to move forward?
   _____
   _____

5. Your life resolution for today:
   "I commit to (action) _____ today, as I move closer to experiencing _____ in my life!"

6. With whom will you share today's life resolution to help hold you accountable?
   _____

EVENING REFLECTION:

Which insights will you take into tomorrow?
_____
_____

Day 135

As we share our fears and pains, we ignite our common bonds. As we share our hopes and happiness, we see just how much we are the same. Today, strengthen humanity. Share a piece of you!

MORNING REFLECTION: Date: _____

1. What is your reflection from today's quote?

2. Into which shoes do you need to step to move forward in this area of your life?

3. Out of which shoes do you need to step that hold you back?

4. What is the one step you can take today to move forward?

5. Your life resolution for today:
   "I commit to (action) _____ today, as I move closer to experiencing _____ in my life!"

6. With whom will you share today's life resolution to help hold you accountable?

EVENING REFLECTION:

Which insights will you take into tomorrow?

Day 136

Our physical human form is not our ends, it is our means—to be that from which we came, and to inspire that in each other. Today, be a means to inspire another.

MORNING REFLECTION: Date: _____

1. What is your reflection from today's quote?

2. Into which shoes do you need to step to move forward in this area of your life?

3. Out of which shoes do you need to step that hold you back?

4. What is the one step you can take today to move forward?

5. Your life resolution for today:
   "I commit to (action) _____ today, as I move closer to experiencing _____ in my life!"

6. With whom will you share today's life resolution to help hold you accountable?

EVENING REFLECTION:

Which insights will you take into tomorrow?

Day 137

All the answers we seek are within us. The key to knowing those answers is to want to know the truths from which we often hide. Today, be fearless in revealing your truths!

MORNING REFLECTION: Date: _____

1. What is your reflection from today's quote?

2. Into which shoes do you need to step to move forward in this area of your life?

3. Out of which shoes do you need to step that hold you back?

4. What is the one step you can take today to move forward?

5. Your life resolution for today:
   "I commit to (action) _____ today, as I move closer to experiencing _____ in my life!"

6. With whom will you share today's life resolution to help hold you accountable?

EVENING REFLECTION:

Which insights will you take into tomorrow?

Day 138

Our day can be filled with complexity and confusion, or simplicity and serenity. We create it by our actions and reactions. Today, be simple.

MORNING REFLECTION: Date: _____

1. What is your reflection from today's quote?
   _____
   _____

2. Into which shoes do you need to step to move forward in this area of your life?
   _____
   _____

3. Out of which shoes do you need to step that hold you back?
   _____
   _____

4. What is the one step you can take today to move forward?
   _____
   _____

5. Your life resolution for today:
   "I commit to (action) _____ today, as I move closer to experiencing _____ in my life!"

6. With whom will you share today's life resolution to help hold you accountable?
   _____

EVENING REFLECTION:

Which insights will you take into tomorrow?
_____

Day 139

There are many things to do, but there are greater things
to be. Today, do the things that allow you to be!

MORNING REFLECTION: Date: _____

1. What is your reflection from today's quote?
   _____
   _____

2. Into which shoes do you need to step to move forward in this area of your life?
   _____
   _____

3. Out of which shoes do you need to step that hold you back?
   _____
   _____

4. What is the one step you can take today to move forward?
   _____
   _____

5. Your life resolution for today:
   "I commit to (action) _____ today, as I
   move closer to experiencing _____ in my life!"

6. With whom will you share today's life resolution to help hold you accountable?
   _____

EVENING REFLECTION:

Which insights will you take into tomorrow?
_____

Day 140

We each experience negative "triggers" from our past, but when we pause and transform those triggers into navigating points, then we discover the positive steps we need to take. Today, allow your triggers to move you forward.

MORNING REFLECTION: Date: _____

1. What is your reflection from today's quote?
   _____
   _____

2. Into which shoes do you need to step to move forward in this area of your life?
   _____
   _____

3. Out of which shoes do you need to step that hold you back?
   _____
   _____

4. What is the one step you can take today to move forward?
   _____
   _____

5. Your life resolution for today:
   "I commit to (action) _____ today, as I move closer to experiencing _____ in my life!"

6. With whom will you share today's life resolution to help hold you accountable?
   _____

EVENING REFLECTION:

Which insights will you take into tomorrow?
_____
_____

Day 141

Those things that "trigger" us become clues as to where we still need to do work, to constantly tune-up, and keep nurturing the weakest parts of us so the whole of us can be strong. Today, pay attention to the clues.

MORNING REFLECTION: Date: _____

1. What is your reflection from today's quote?

2. Into which shoes do you need to step to move forward in this area of your life?

3. Out of which shoes do you need to step that hold you back?

4. What is the one step you can take today to move forward?

5. Your life resolution for today:
   "I commit to (action) _____ today, as I move closer to experiencing _____ in my life!"

6. With whom will you share today's life resolution to help hold you accountable?

EVENING REFLECTION:

Which insights will you take into tomorrow?

Day 142

The key to transitioning through the portals of life is often not found along the paths of certainty, but amidst the currents of uncertainty, toward unknown destinations. Today, walk through uncertainty to discovery.

MORNING REFLECTION: Date: _____

1. What is your reflection from today's quote?

2. Into which shoes do you need to step to move forward in this area of your life?

3. Out of which shoes do you need to step that hold you back?

4. What is the one step you can take today to move forward?

5. Your life resolution for today:
   "I commit to (action) _____ today, as I move closer to experiencing _____ in my life!"

6. With whom will you share today's life resolution to help hold you accountable?

EVENING REFLECTION:

Which insights will you take into tomorrow?

Day 143

You have the power to imagine the greatest masterpiece you could wish to create with your life. So too, you have the power to make it real. Today, make it real.

MORNING REFLECTION: Date: _____

1. What is your reflection from today's quote?

2. Into which shoes do you need to step to move forward in this area of your life?

3. Out of which shoes do you need to step that hold you back?

4. What is the one step you can take today to move forward?

5. Your life resolution for today:
   "I commit to (action) _____ today, as I move closer to experiencing _____ in my life!"

6. With whom will you share today's life resolution to help hold you accountable?

EVENING REFLECTION:

Which insights will you take into tomorrow?

Day 144

We can throw our clothes into the wind, we can lay naked in the sun, we can expose every atom of our being in the world around. We can be free to "be" all that we are. Today, be naked.

MORNING REFLECTION: Date: _____

1. What is your reflection from today's quote?
   _____
   _____

2. Into which shoes do you need to step to move forward in this area of your life?
   _____

3. Out of which shoes do you need to step that hold you back?
   _____

4. What is the one step you can take today to move forward?
   _____

5. Your life resolution for today:
   "I commit to (action) _____ today, as I move closer to experiencing _____ in my life!"

6. With whom will you share today's life resolution to help hold you accountable?
   _____

EVENING REFLECTION:

Which insights will you take into tomorrow?
_____
_____

Day 145

We find in each moment, that which we seek to find.
Today, seek and find.

MORNING REFLECTION: Date:

1. What is your reflection from today's quote?

2. Into which shoes do you need to step to move forward in this area of your life?

3. Out of which shoes do you need to step that hold you back?

4. What is the one step you can take today to move forward?

5. Your life resolution for today:
   "I commit to (action) _____ today, as I move closer to experiencing _____ in my life!"

6. With whom will you share today's life resolution to help hold you accountable?

EVENING REFLECTION:

Which insights will you take into tomorrow?

Day 146

Our ability to take flight is only limited by how far we wish to soar toward the sky. Today, let yourself soar.

MORNING REFLECTION: Date: _____

1. What is your reflection from today's quote?

2. Into which shoes do you need to step to move forward in this area of your life?

3. Out of which shoes do you need to step that hold you back?

4. What is the one step you can take today to move forward?

5. Your life resolution for today:
   "I commit to (action) _____ today, as I move closer to experiencing _____ in my life!"

6. With whom will you share today's life resolution to help hold you accountable?

EVENING REFLECTION:

Which insights will you take into tomorrow?

Day 147

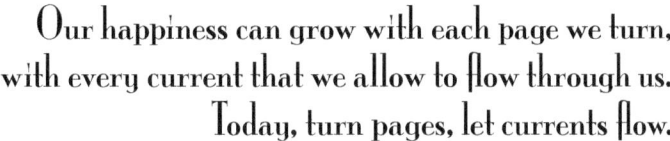
Our happiness can grow with each page we turn,
with every current that we allow to flow through us.
Today, turn pages, let currents flow.

MORNING REFLECTION: Date: _____

1. What is your reflection from today's quote?
   _____
   _____

2. Into which shoes do you need to step to move forward in this area of your life?
   _____
   _____

3. Out of which shoes do you need to step that hold you back?
   _____
   _____

4. What is the one step you can take today to move forward?
   _____
   _____

5. Your life resolution for today:
   "I commit to (action) _____ today, as I
   move closer to experiencing _____ in my life!"

6. With whom will you share today's life resolution to help hold you accountable?
   _____

EVENING REFLECTION:

Which insights will you take into tomorrow?
_____
_____

Day 148

When we forgive ourselves, and show ourselves kindness and compassion, rather than punishing ourselves, we set ourselves free. Today, be compassionate and kind to yourself. Set yourself free.

MORNING REFLECTION: Date: _____

1. What is your reflection from today's quote?

2. Into which shoes do you need to step to move forward in this area of your life?

3. Out of which shoes do you need to step that hold you back?

4. What is the one step you can take today to move forward?

5. Your life resolution for today:
   "I commit to (action) _____ today, as I move closer to experiencing _____ in my life!"

6. With whom will you share today's life resolution to help hold you accountable?

EVENING REFLECTION:

Which insights will you take into tomorrow?

Day 149

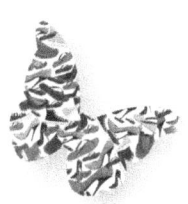

We have the forces of good standing ready to overcome the forces of evil. We have our defenders and our heroes waiting to be summoned who can form an army to conquer our greatest challenges. Today, summon your army.

MORNING REFLECTION: Date:

1. What is your reflection from today's quote?

2. Into which shoes do you need to step to move forward in this area of your life?

3. Out of which shoes do you need to step that hold you back?

4. What is the one step you can take today to move forward?

5. Your life resolution for today:
   "I commit to (action) _____ today, as I move closer to experiencing _____ in my life!"

6. With whom will you share today's life resolution to help hold you accountable?

EVENING REFLECTION:

Which insights will you take into tomorrow?

Day 150

We can transform the negative energy of pain that traps us, into the positive energy that moves us forward.
Today, move forward.

MORNING REFLECTION: Date: _____

1. What is your reflection from today's quote?

2. Into which shoes do you need to step to move forward in this area of your life?

3. Out of which shoes do you need to step that hold you back?

4. What is the one step you can take today to move forward?

5. Your life resolution for today:
   "I commit to (action) _____ today, as I move closer to experiencing _____ in my life!"

6. With whom will you share today's life resolution to help hold you accountable?

EVENING REFLECTION:

Which insights will you take into tomorrow?

Day 151

The opportunities to allow healing and rejuvenating currents to flow through us are all around. Every day, we don't need to journey far to feel the life force that constantly flows around and through us. Today, feel your force.

MORNING REFLECTION: Date: _____

1. What is your reflection from today's quote?

2. Into which shoes do you need to step to move forward in this area of your life?

3. Out of which shoes do you need to step that hold you back?

4. What is the one step you can take today to move forward?

5. Your life resolution for today:
   "I commit to (action) _____ today, as I move closer to experiencing _____ in my life!"

6. With whom will you share today's life resolution to help hold you accountable?

EVENING REFLECTION:

Which insights will you take into tomorrow?

Day 152

More than anything, we are what we think.
Today, think extraordinarily.

MORNING REFLECTION: Date: _____

1. What is your reflection from today's quote?
   _____
   _____

2. Into which shoes do you need to step to move forward in this area of your life?
   _____

3. Out of which shoes do you need to step that hold you back?
   _____

4. What is the one step you can take today to move forward?
   _____

5. Your life resolution for today:
   "I commit to (action) _____ today, as I move closer to experiencing _____ in my life!"

6. With whom will you share today's life resolution to help hold you accountable?
   _____

EVENING REFLECTION:

Which insights will you take into tomorrow?
_____

Day 153

Our lives can be an abundance of extraordinary creations, with one leading to another as we evolve with each creation. Each new day brings a new canvas upon which we can create a more abundant and authentic scene. Today, create your most extraordinary scene.

MORNING REFLECTION: Date: _____

1. What is your reflection from today's quote?
   _____
   _____

2. Into which shoes do you need to step to move forward in this area of your life?
   _____
   _____

3. Out of which shoes do you need to step that hold you back?
   _____
   _____

4. What is the one step you can take today to move forward?
   _____
   _____

5. Your life resolution for today:
   "I commit to (action) _____ today, as I move closer to experiencing _____ in my life!"

6. With whom will you share today's life resolution to help hold you accountable?
   _____

EVENING REFLECTION:

Which insights will you take into tomorrow?
_____
_____

Day 154

When we change our shoes and walk in the shoes of another, we not only change our lives, but also change the lives of those around us. We can start to change the world. Today, walk in the shoes of another.

MORNING REFLECTION: Date: _____

1. What is your reflection from today's quote?

2. Into which shoes do you need to step to move forward in this area of your life?

3. Out of which shoes do you need to step that hold you back?

4. What is the one step you can take today to move forward?

5. Your life resolution for today:
   "I commit to (action) _____ today, as I move closer to experiencing _____ in my life!"

6. With whom will you share today's life resolution to help hold you accountable?

EVENING REFLECTION:

Which insights will you take into tomorrow?

Day 155

Within each of us, amidst the gray that invariably finds its way to us, are fields of green that emerge to create beautiful and renewed landscapes. Today, lay yourself down in your fields of green.

MORNING REFLECTION: Date:

1. What is your reflection from today's quote?

2. Into which shoes do you need to step to move forward in this area of your life?

3. Out of which shoes do you need to step that hold you back?

4. What is the one step you can take today to move forward?

5. Your life resolution for today:
   "I commit to (action) _____ today, as I move closer to experiencing _____ in my life!"

6. With whom will you share today's life resolution to help hold you accountable?

EVENING REFLECTION:

Which insights will you take into tomorrow?

Day 156

On the edge, there is imminent danger, but there is also vast discovery. Today, step out and experience life on the edge.

MORNING REFLECTION:　　　　　　Date: _____

1. What is your reflection from today's quote?
   _____

2. Into which shoes do you need to step to move forward in this area of your life?
   _____

3. Out of which shoes do you need to step that hold you back?
   _____

4. What is the one step you can take today to move forward?
   _____

5. Your life resolution for today:
   "I commit to (action) _____ today, as I move closer to experiencing _____ in my life!"

6. With whom will you share today's life resolution to help hold you accountable?
   _____

EVENING REFLECTION:

Which insights will you take into tomorrow?
_____

Day 157

Keep listening to all that is within you—that is your guide.
It will grow with each breath and with each pause—and that
is all you need. Today, listen to the answers within you.

MORNING REFLECTION: Date:

1. What is your reflection from today's quote?

2. Into which shoes do you need to step to move forward in this area of your life?

3. Out of which shoes do you need to step that hold you back?

4. What is the one step you can take today to move forward?

5. Your life resolution for today:
   "I commit to (action) _____ today, as I move closer to experiencing _____ in my life!"

6. With whom will you share today's life resolution to help hold you accountable?

EVENING REFLECTION:

Which insights will you take into tomorrow?

Day 158

The journeys of our lives are a product of how we think—about ourselves, about each other, about the world. Today, think without limits.

MORNING REFLECTION: Date: _____

1. What is your reflection from today's quote?
   _____
   _____

2. Into which shoes do you need to step to move forward in this area of your life?
   _____
   _____

3. Out of which shoes do you need to step that hold you back?
   _____
   _____

4. What is the one step you can take today to move forward?
   _____
   _____

5. Your life resolution for today:
   "I commit to (action) _____ today, as I move closer to experiencing _____ in my life!"

6. With whom will you share today's life resolution to help hold you accountable?
   _____

EVENING REFLECTION:

Which insights will you take into tomorrow?
_____
_____

Day 159

Extraordinary, "breakthrough" moments are created when we are daring enough to put ourselves on the line; when we confront our greatest fears; step into the most uncomfortable parts of ourselves and simply stand there and feel our authentic presence in every part of us. Today, create breakthrough moments.

MORNING REFLECTION: Date: _____

1. What is your reflection from today's quote?

2. Into which shoes do you need to step to move forward in this area of your life?

3. Out of which shoes do you need to step that hold you back?

4. What is the one step you can take today to move forward?

5. Your life resolution for today:
   "I commit to (action) _____ today, as I move closer to experiencing _____ in my life!"

6. With whom will you share today's life resolution to help hold you accountable?

EVENING REFLECTION:

Which insights will you take into tomorrow?

Day 160

We each have the power to step into our greatest selves—it is in our nature—it is a part of the masterpiece of the human spirit. It simply takes a first step. Today, step into your nature.

MORNING REFLECTION: Date: _____

1. What is your reflection from today's quote?

2. Into which shoes do you need to step to move forward in this area of your life?

3. Out of which shoes do you need to step that hold you back?

4. What is the one step you can take today to move forward?

5. Your life resolution for today:
   "I commit to (action) _____ today, as I move closer to experiencing _____ in my life!"

6. With whom will you share today's life resolution to help hold you accountable?

EVENING REFLECTION:

Which insights will you take into tomorrow?

Day 161

We feel when our internal compass is resonating on
its True North, sending vibrations through us.
Today, pause and be guided by your compass within.

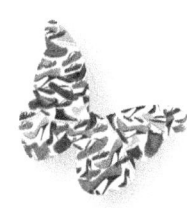

MORNING REFLECTION: Date: _____

1. What is your reflection from today's quote?
   _____
   _____

2. Into which shoes do you need to step to move forward in this area of your life?
   _____
   _____

3. Out of which shoes do you need to step that hold you back?
   _____
   _____

4. What is the one step you can take today to move forward?
   _____
   _____

5. Your life resolution for today:
   "I commit to (action) _____ today, as I
   move closer to experiencing _____ in my life!"

6. With whom will you share today's life resolution to help hold you accountable?
   _____

EVENING REFLECTION:

Which insights will you take into tomorrow?
_____
_____

Day 162

Doors open before us every day.
Today, take one step into a door to your dreams.

MORNING REFLECTION: Date: _____

1. What is your reflection from today's quote?
   _____
   _____

2. Into which shoes do you need to step to move forward in this area of your life?
   _____
   _____

3. Out of which shoes do you need to step that hold you back?
   _____
   _____

4. What is the one step you can take today to move forward?
   _____
   _____

5. Your life resolution for today:
   "I commit to (action) _____ today, as I
   move closer to experiencing _____ in my life!"

6. With whom will you share today's life resolution to help hold you accountable?
   _____

EVENING REFLECTION:

Which insights will you take into tomorrow?
_____

Day 163

The deeper you excavate into your "self," the more room
you create to pour the pillars that will hold you high.
Today, dig deeper, feel stronger, rise higher.

MORNING REFLECTION: Date: _____

1. What is your reflection from today's quote?
   _____
   _____

2. Into which shoes do you need to step to move forward in this area of your life?
   _____

3. Out of which shoes do you need to step that hold you back?
   _____
   _____

4. What is the one step you can take today to move forward?
   _____

5. Your life resolution for today:
   "I commit to (action) _____ today, as I
   move closer to experiencing _____ in my life!"

6. With whom will you share today's life resolution to help hold you accountable?
   _____

EVENING REFLECTION:

Which insights will you take into tomorrow?
_____
_____

Day 164

We can activate every atom of our being with an intentional thought that sparks our transformation. Today, create intentional thoughts.

MORNING REFLECTION: Date: _____

1. What is your reflection from today's quote?
   _____
   _____

2. Into which shoes do you need to step to move forward in this area of your life?
   _____
   _____

3. Out of which shoes do you need to step that hold you back?
   _____
   _____

4. What is the one step you can take today to move forward?
   _____
   _____

5. Your life resolution for today:
   "I commit to (action) _____ today, as I move closer to experiencing _____ in my life!"

6. With whom will you share today's life resolution to help hold you accountable?
   _____

EVENING REFLECTION:

Which insights will you take into tomorrow?
_____
_____

Day 165

You need to treat your "self" as your greatest gift.
You need to be good to your "self" in order for good to emerge.
Today, spoil your "self" abundantly.

MORNING REFLECTION: Date:

1. What is your reflection from today's quote?

2. Into which shoes do you need to step to move forward in this area of your life?

3. Out of which shoes do you need to step that hold you back?

4. What is the one step you can take today to move forward?

5. Your life resolution for today:
   "I commit to (action) _____ today, as I move closer to experiencing _____ in my life!"

6. With whom will you share today's life resolution to help hold you accountable?

EVENING REFLECTION:

Which insights will you take into tomorrow?

Day 166

We are a seed of creation.
Today, grow!

MORNING REFLECTION: Date: _____

1. What is your reflection from today's quote?

2. Into which shoes do you need to step to move forward in this area of your life?

3. Out of which shoes do you need to step that hold you back?

4. What is the one step you can take today to move forward?

5. Your life resolution for today:
   "I commit to (action) _____ today, as I move closer to experiencing _____ in my life!"

6. With whom will you share today's life resolution to help hold you accountable?

EVENING REFLECTION:

Which insights will you take into tomorrow?

Day 167

We can catapult to our greatest heights, move through our most turbulent waters, capture our most purposeful pursuits, reach further than what appears before us, and boldly venture into the wondrous mystery of tomorrow. Today, allow your most powerful presence to move you.

MORNING REFLECTION: Date: _____

1. What is your reflection from today's quote?
   _____
   _____

2. Into which shoes do you need to step to move forward in this area of your life?
   _____
   _____

3. Out of which shoes do you need to step that hold you back?
   _____
   _____

4. What is the one step you can take today to move forward?
   _____
   _____

5. Your life resolution for today:
   "I commit to (action) _____ today, as I move closer to experiencing _____ in my life!"

6. With whom will you share today's life resolution to help hold you accountable?
   _____

EVENING REFLECTION:

Which insights will you take into tomorrow?
_____
_____

Day 168

The future we create starts with the steps we take in this moment. Today, choose your step!

MORNING REFLECTION: Date: _____

1. What is your reflection from today's quote?
   _____
   _____

2. Into which shoes do you need to step to move forward in this area of your life?
   _____
   _____

3. Out of which shoes do you need to step that hold you back?
   _____
   _____

4. What is the one step you can take today to move forward?
   _____
   _____

5. Your life resolution for today:
   "I commit to (action) _____ today, as I move closer to experiencing _____ in my life!"

6. With whom will you share today's life resolution to help hold you accountable?
   _____

EVENING REFLECTION:

Which insights will you take into tomorrow?
_____
_____

Day 169

You can empower your "self."
Today, give your "self" all the power you need!

MORNING REFLECTION: Date: _____

1. What is your reflection from today's quote?

2. Into which shoes do you need to step to move forward in this area of your life?

3. Out of which shoes do you need to step that hold you back?

4. What is the one step you can take today to move forward?

5. Your life resolution for today:
   "I commit to (action) _____ today, as I move closer to experiencing _____ in my life!"

6. With whom will you share today's life resolution to help hold you accountable?

EVENING REFLECTION:

Which insights will you take into tomorrow?

Day 170

We can move mountains far from us, close to us, and within us.
We simply need to believe we can. Today, believe, and move mountains.

MORNING REFLECTION: Date: _____

1. What is your reflection from today's quote?

2. Into which shoes do you need to step to move forward in this area of your life?

3. Out of which shoes do you need to step that hold you back?

4. What is the one step you can take today to move forward?

5. Your life resolution for today:
   "I commit to (action) _____ today, as I move closer to experiencing _____ in my life!"

6. With whom will you share today's life resolution to help hold you accountable?

EVENING REFLECTION:

Which insights will you take into tomorrow?

Day 171

You need to care for all of the parts of your "self"—for your body, your mind, and your spirit—in order to conquer your demons, in order for your soul to fill your being. Today, care for you.

MORNING REFLECTION: Date: _____

1. What is your reflection from today's quote?
   _____
   _____

2. Into which shoes do you need to step to move forward in this area of your life?
   _____
   _____

3. Out of which shoes do you need to step that hold you back?
   _____
   _____

4. What is the one step you can take today to move forward?
   _____
   _____

5. Your life resolution for today:
   "I commit to (action) _____ today, as I move closer to experiencing _____ in my life!"

6. With whom will you share today's life resolution to help hold you accountable?
   _____

EVENING REFLECTION:

Which insights will you take into tomorrow?
_____
_____

Day 172

Instead of standing silent knowing others are still isolated prisoners in their pain, we can stand together and rise until every person is standing tall. Today, rise for yourself. Rise for another!

MORNING REFLECTION: Date: _____

1. What is your reflection from today's quote?
   _____

2. Into which shoes do you need to step to move forward in this area of your life?
   _____

3. Out of which shoes do you need to step that hold you back?
   _____

4. What is the one step you can take today to move forward?
   _____

5. Your life resolution for today:
   "I commit to (action) _____ today, as I move closer to experiencing _____ in my life!"

6. With whom will you share today's life resolution to help hold you accountable?
   _____

EVENING REFLECTION:

Which insights will you take into tomorrow?
_____

Day 173

In each moment, we have access to qualities that help us to create balance and harmony, or to create chaos and disruption. The power is within us. Today, choose to create balance and harmony.

MORNING REFLECTION: Date:

1. What is your reflection from today's quote?

2. Into which shoes do you need to step to move forward in this area of your life?

3. Out of which shoes do you need to step that hold you back?

4. What is the one step you can take today to move forward?

5. Your life resolution for today:
   "I commit to (action) _____ today, as I move closer to experiencing _____ in my life!"

6. With whom will you share today's life resolution to help hold you accountable?

EVENING REFLECTION:

Which insights will you take into tomorrow?

Day 174

We need to summon the extraordinary power that lies within us in order to be the greatest power we can be. Today, summon your greatest powers loudly and passionately!

MORNING REFLECTION: Date: _____

1. What is your reflection from today's quote?

2. Into which shoes do you need to step to move forward in this area of your life?

3. Out of which shoes do you need to step that hold you back?

4. What is the one step you can take today to move forward?

5. Your life resolution for today:
   "I commit to (action) _____ today, as I move closer to experiencing _____ in my life!"

6. With whom will you share today's life resolution to help hold you accountable?

EVENING REFLECTION:

Which insights will you take into tomorrow?

Day 175

The sun rises, ever present through the day, nurturing, transforming, even if it cannot be seen. Today, feel the sun that rises within you.

MORNING REFLECTION: Date: _____

1. What is your reflection from today's quote?

2. Into which shoes do you need to step to move forward in this area of your life?

3. Out of which shoes do you need to step that hold you back?

4. What is the one step you can take today to move forward?

5. Your life resolution for today:
   "I commit to (action) _____ today, as I move closer to experiencing _____ in my life!"

6. With whom will you share today's life resolution to help hold you accountable?

EVENING REFLECTION:

Which insights will you take into tomorrow?

Day 176

We each have our stories, each as significant as the next, each able to make a connection to another.
Today, make a connection to another.

MORNING REFLECTION: Date: _____

1. What is your reflection from today's quote?
   _____
   _____

2. Into which shoes do you need to step to move forward in this area of your life?
   _____

3. Out of which shoes do you need to step that hold you back?
   _____

4. What is the one step you can take today to move forward?
   _____

5. Your life resolution for today:
   "I commit to (action) _____ today, as I
   move closer to experiencing _____ in my life!"

6. With whom will you share today's life resolution to help hold you accountable?
   _____

EVENING REFLECTION:

Which insights will you take into tomorrow?
_____
_____

Day 177

Once we tap into the vast ocean of our limitless potential,
we discover new depths and powerful forces.
Today, dive into your ocean.

MORNING REFLECTION: Date: _____

1. What is your reflection from today's quote?
   _____
   _____

2. Into which shoes do you need to step to move forward in this area of your life?
   _____
   _____

3. Out of which shoes do you need to step that hold you back?
   _____
   _____

4. What is the one step you can take today to move forward?
   _____
   _____

5. Your life resolution for today:
   "I commit to (action) _____ today, as I
   move closer to experiencing _____ in my life!"

6. With whom will you share today's life resolution to help hold you accountable?

EVENING REFLECTION:

Which insights will you take into tomorrow?
_____
_____

Day 178

When we feel the freedom to choose to step into whichever shoes we desire, we start to transform our reality. Today, transform your reality.

MORNING REFLECTION: Date: _____

1. What is your reflection from today's quote?
   _____
   _____

2. Into which shoes do you need to step to move forward in this area of your life?
   _____
   _____

3. Out of which shoes do you need to step that hold you back?
   _____
   _____

4. What is the one step you can take today to move forward?
   _____
   _____

5. Your life resolution for today:
   "I commit to (action) _____ today, as I move closer to experiencing _____ in my life!"

6. With whom will you share today's life resolution to help hold you accountable?
   _____

EVENING REFLECTION:

Which insights will you take into tomorrow?
_____
_____

Day 179

When we pause in the resonance of the compass within, and see the light of the North Star guiding us, we discover new paths that are uniquely ours. Today, discover your unique paths.

MORNING REFLECTION: Date: _____

1. What is your reflection from today's quote?

2. Into which shoes do you need to step to move forward in this area of your life?

3. Out of which shoes do you need to step that hold you back?

4. What is the one step you can take today to move forward?

5. Your life resolution for today:
   "I commit to (action) _____ today, as I move closer to experiencing _____ in my life!"

6. With whom will you share today's life resolution to help hold you accountable?

EVENING REFLECTION:

Which insights will you take into tomorrow?

Day 180

We are here to create intricate masterpieces of our lives, to be inspired by new influences that make us more distinctive and unique with each brush stroke. Today, be inspired.

MORNING REFLECTION: Date: _____

1. What is your reflection from today's quote?

2. Into which shoes do you need to step to move forward in this area of your life?

3. Out of which shoes do you need to step that hold you back?

4. What is the one step you can take today to move forward?

5. Your life resolution for today:
   "I commit to (action) _____ today, as I move closer to experiencing _____ in my life!"

6. With whom will you share today's life resolution to help hold you accountable?

EVENING REFLECTION:

Which insights will you take into tomorrow?

Day 181

We must believe we can move mountains, before the soil will start to shift. When we believe enough, we can cause a landslide. We can displace the earth. Mountains will move. Today, believe more!

MORNING REFLECTION: Date:

1. What is your reflection from today's quote?

2. Into which shoes do you need to step to move forward in this area of your life?

3. Out of which shoes do you need to step that hold you back?

4. What is the one step you can take today to move forward?

5. Your life resolution for today:
   "I commit to (action) _____ today, as I move closer to experiencing _____ in my life!"

6. With whom will you share today's life resolution to help hold you accountable?

EVENING REFLECTION:

Which insights will you take into tomorrow?

Day 182

Within each first step, there is always doubt and fear, but if we let the sense of freedom and opportunity overcome the fear, all else will follow. Today, step into your fear.

MORNING REFLECTION: Date: _____

1. What is your reflection from today's quote?

2. Into which shoes do you need to step to move forward in this area of your life?

3. Out of which shoes do you need to step that hold you back?

4. What is the one step you can take today to move forward?

5. Your life resolution for today:
   "I commit to (action) _____ today, as I move closer to experiencing _____ in my life!"

6. With whom will you share today's life resolution to help hold you accountable?

EVENING REFLECTION:

Which insights will you take into tomorrow?

Day 183

We can get stuck in the role of victim and feel at the mercy of all that is around, rather than feel we have the strength to break free. Today, tap into the infinite strength within you. Break free!

MORNING REFLECTION: Date: _____

1. What is your reflection from today's quote?

2. Into which shoes do you need to step to move forward in this area of your life?

3. Out of which shoes do you need to step that hold you back?

4. What is the one step you can take today to move forward?

5. Your life resolution for today:
   "I commit to (action) _____ today, as I move closer to experiencing _____ in my life!"

6. With whom will you share today's life resolution to help hold you accountable?

EVENING REFLECTION:

Which insights will you take into tomorrow?

Day 184

To move beyond the things that hold us back, to pursue all that is important to us, we need to give voice to the things that keep us silent. Your voice can be your momentum. Today, free your voice.

MORNING REFLECTION: Date: _____

1. What is your reflection from today's quote?

2. Into which shoes do you need to step to move forward in this area of your life?

3. Out of which shoes do you need to step that hold you back?

4. What is the one step you can take today to move forward?

5. Your life resolution for today:
   "I commit to (action) _____ today, as I move closer to experiencing _____ in my life!"

6. With whom will you share today's life resolution to help hold you accountable?

EVENING REFLECTION:

Which insights will you take into tomorrow?

Day 185

Life is an ocean of stepping stones that take us to our farthest horizons. Today, leap into your horizons!

MORNING REFLECTION: Date:

1. What is your reflection from today's quote?

2. Into which shoes do you need to step to move forward in this area of your life?

3. Out of which shoes do you need to step that hold you back?

4. What is the one step you can take today to move forward?

5. Your life resolution for today:
   "I commit to (action) _____ today, as I move closer to experiencing _____ in my life!"

6. With whom will you share today's life resolution to help hold you accountable?

EVENING REFLECTION:

Which insights will you take into tomorrow?

Day 186

Sometimes, "just living" is all that we feel we can do. Yet, beyond "just living" is a life of dreams. Today, stay in the power of your dreams.

MORNING REFLECTION: Date: _____

1. What is your reflection from today's quote?

2. Into which shoes do you need to step to move forward in this area of your life?

3. Out of which shoes do you need to step that hold you back?

4. What is the one step you can take today to move forward?

5. Your life resolution for today:
   "I commit to (action) _____ today, as I move closer to experiencing _____ in my life!"

6. With whom will you share today's life resolution to help hold you accountable?

EVENING REFLECTION:

Which insights will you take into tomorrow?

Day 187

When we allow the currents of love and laughter to flow through us, we can dilute the poison of our pain. Today, allow purifying currents to flow through you and live renewed.

MORNING REFLECTION: Date: _____

1. What is your reflection from today's quote?

2. Into which shoes do you need to step to move forward in this area of your life?

3. Out of which shoes do you need to step that hold you back?

4. What is the one step you can take today to move forward?

5. Your life resolution for today:
   "I commit to (action) _____ today, as I move closer to experiencing _____ in my life!"

6. With whom will you share today's life resolution to help hold you accountable?

EVENING REFLECTION:

Which insights will you take into tomorrow?

Day 188

If we dare, we can allow the touch of the universe to shine light onto parts of ourselves that have been lost in our darkness. Today, turn on the light within you and reveal your greatest self.

MORNING REFLECTION: Date:

1. What is your reflection from today's quote?

2. Into which shoes do you need to step to move forward in this area of your life?

3. Out of which shoes do you need to step that hold you back?

4. What is the one step you can take today to move forward?

5. Your life resolution for today:
   "I commit to (action) _____ today, as I move closer to experiencing _____ in my life!"

6. With whom will you share today's life resolution to help hold you accountable?

EVENING REFLECTION:

Which insights will you take into tomorrow?

Day 189

In order to dig deep and excavate the pieces of your "self" that no longer serve you, you need to know the deepest and most hidden parts of your "self." Today, explore your depths, and discover your heights.

MORNING REFLECTION: Date: _____

1. What is your reflection from today's quote?
   _____
   _____

2. Into which shoes do you need to step to move forward in this area of your life?
   _____
   _____

3. Out of which shoes do you need to step that hold you back?
   _____
   _____

4. What is the one step you can take today to move forward?
   _____
   _____

5. Your life resolution for today:
   "I commit to (action) _____ today, as I move closer to experiencing _____ in my life!"

6. With whom will you share today's life resolution to help hold you accountable?

EVENING REFLECTION:

Which insights will you take into tomorrow?
_____
_____

Day 190

You have it within you to turn your life into your masterpiece. Today, step into the masterpiece of you!

MORNING REFLECTION: Date: _____

1. What is your reflection from today's quote?
   _____
   _____

2. Into which shoes do you need to step to move forward in this area of your life?
   _____
   _____

3. Out of which shoes do you need to step that hold you back?
   _____
   _____

4. What is the one step you can take today to move forward?
   _____
   _____

5. Your life resolution for today:
   "I commit to (action) _____ today, as I move closer to experiencing _____ in my life!"

6. With whom will you share today's life resolution to help hold you accountable?
   _____

EVENING REFLECTION:

Which insights will you take into tomorrow?
_____

Day 191

If we don't walk the next step, we will never know what
is just around the corner. Today, keep walking.

MORNING REFLECTION: Date: _____

1. What is your reflection from today's quote?
   _____
   _____

2. Into which shoes do you need to step to move forward in this area of your life?
   _____
   _____

3. Out of which shoes do you need to step that hold you back?
   _____
   _____

4. What is the one step you can take today to move forward?
   _____
   _____

5. Your life resolution for today:
   "I commit to (action) _____ today, as I
   move closer to experiencing _____ in my life!"

6. With whom will you share today's life resolution to help hold you accountable?
   _____

EVENING REFLECTION:

Which insights will you take into tomorrow?
_____
_____

Day 192

Once we start to care for ourselves, we can conquer the things that keep us from being kind and good to us. Today, conquer your "self" with kindness!

MORNING REFLECTION: Date: _____

1. What is your reflection from today's quote?

2. Into which shoes do you need to step to move forward in this area of your life?

3. Out of which shoes do you need to step that hold you back?

4. What is the one step you can take today to move forward?

5. Your life resolution for today:
   "I commit to (action) _____ today, as I move closer to experiencing _____ in my life!"

6. With whom will you share today's life resolution to help hold you accountable?

EVENING REFLECTION:

Which insights will you take into tomorrow?

Day 193

All that you need to create an epic life is with you now in this present moment. You simply need to step into it. Today, imagine how epic your life can be and step into it!

MORNING REFLECTION: Date:

1. What is your reflection from today's quote?

2. Into which shoes do you need to step to move forward in this area of your life?

3. Out of which shoes do you need to step that hold you back?

4. What is the one step you can take today to move forward?

5. Your life resolution for today:
   "I commit to (action) _____ today, as I move closer to experiencing _____ in my life!"

6. With whom will you share today's life resolution to help hold you accountable?

EVENING REFLECTION:

Which insights will you take into tomorrow?

Day 194

Whichever spirit, God, essence, or divine being resonates within each of us, that presence speaks to us in each moment. Today, pause and hear the divinity within you.

MORNING REFLECTION: Date: _____

1. What is your reflection from today's quote?

2. Into which shoes do you need to step to move forward in this area of your life?

3. Out of which shoes do you need to step that hold you back?

4. What is the one step you can take today to move forward?

5. Your life resolution for today:
   "I commit to (action) _____ today, as I move closer to experiencing _____ in my life!"

6. With whom will you share today's life resolution to help hold you accountable?

EVENING REFLECTION:

Which insights will you take into tomorrow?

Day 195

We don't need to continually look beyond ourselves to make the right choices on our journeys. We need to look and feel within ourselves. Today, make choices from within yourself.

MORNING REFLECTION: Date: _____

1. What is your reflection from today's quote?

2. Into which shoes do you need to step to move forward in this area of your life?

3. Out of which shoes do you need to step that hold you back?

4. What is the one step you can take today to move forward?

5. Your life resolution for today:
   "I commit to (action) _____ today, as I move closer to experiencing _____ in my life!"

6. With whom will you share today's life resolution to help hold you accountable?

EVENING REFLECTION:

Which insights will you take into tomorrow?

Day 196

The more we live each moment being present in the "everything" of that moment, the more we tap into our unlimited power. Today, live in the "everything" of the moment.

MORNING REFLECTION: Date: _____

1. What is your reflection from today's quote?

2. Into which shoes do you need to step to move forward in this area of your life?

3. Out of which shoes do you need to step that hold you back?

4. What is the one step you can take today to move forward?

5. Your life resolution for today:
   "I commit to (action) _____ today, as I move closer to experiencing _____ in my life!"

6. With whom will you share today's life resolution to help hold you accountable?

EVENING REFLECTION:

Which insights will you take into tomorrow?

Day 197

We can reach within and touch the power of
our creation. Today, reach within.

MORNING REFLECTION: Date:

1. What is your reflection from today's quote?

2. Into which shoes do you need to step to move forward in this area of your life?

3. Out of which shoes do you need to step that hold you back?

4. What is the one step you can take today to move forward?

5. Your life resolution for today:
   "I commit to (action) _____ today, as I
   move closer to experiencing _____ in my life!"

6. With whom will you share today's life resolution to help hold you accountable?

EVENING REFLECTION:

Which insights will you take into tomorrow?

Day 198

We can come so close to enabling someone else to cause us to give up. We forget that our next step forward is completely in our own hands. Today, take your "self" into your own hands.

MORNING REFLECTION: Date: _____

1. What is your reflection from today's quote?
   _____
   _____

2. Into which shoes do you need to step to move forward in this area of your life?
   _____
   _____

3. Out of which shoes do you need to step that hold you back?
   _____
   _____

4. What is the one step you can take today to move forward?
   _____
   _____

5. Your life resolution for today:
   "I commit to (action) _____ today, as I move closer to experiencing _____ in my life!"

6. With whom will you share today's life resolution to help hold you accountable?
   _____

EVENING REFLECTION:

Which insights will you take into tomorrow?
_____
_____

Day 199

We can transcend our negative thoughts, rise above the worst that has happened to us, and connect with our unique purpose that lies within us. Today, let your purpose overcome your pain.

MORNING REFLECTION: Date: _____

1. What is your reflection from today's quote?

2. Into which shoes do you need to step to move forward in this area of your life?

3. Out of which shoes do you need to step that hold you back?

4. What is the one step you can take today to move forward?

5. Your life resolution for today:
   "I commit to (action) _____ today, as I move closer to experiencing _____ in my life!"

6. With whom will you share today's life resolution to help hold you accountable?

EVENING REFLECTION:

Which insights will you take into tomorrow?

Day 200

You can take charge of your story. You have the choice. You can keep it a secret, you can tell it with guilt and shame, or you can tell it with pride and resilience, having risen through it. Your words can set you free. Your words can help others to be free. Today, take charge of your story.

MORNING REFLECTION: Date: _____

1. What is your reflection from today's quote?
   _____
   _____

2. Into which shoes do you need to step to move forward in this area of your life?
   _____
   _____

3. Out of which shoes do you need to step that hold you back?
   _____
   _____

4. What is the one step you can take today to move forward?
   _____
   _____

5. Your life resolution for today:
   "I commit to (action) _____ today, as I move closer to experiencing _____ in my life!"

6. With whom will you share today's life resolution to help hold you accountable?
   _____

EVENING REFLECTION:

Which insights will you take into tomorrow?
_____

Day 201

At the times when you feel the most empty, you can start to see the greatest possibilities to fill your "self" with extraordinary new things. Today, see holes of emptiness as mountains of possibility!

MORNING REFLECTION: Date: _____

1. What is your reflection from today's quote?
   _____
   _____

2. Into which shoes do you need to step to move forward in this area of your life?
   _____
   _____

3. Out of which shoes do you need to step that hold you back?
   _____
   _____

4. What is the one step you can take today to move forward?
   _____
   _____

5. Your life resolution for today:
   "I commit to (action) _____ today, as I move closer to experiencing _____ in my life!"

6. With whom will you share today's life resolution to help hold you accountable?
   _____

EVENING REFLECTION:

Which insights will you take into tomorrow?
_____
_____

Day 202

We can get stuck in the role of victim, and feel at the mercy of all that is around, rather than feel that we have the strength to break free. Today, draw on your strength. You have it. Break free!

MORNING REFLECTION: Date: _____

1. What is your reflection from today's quote?
   _____
   _____

2. Into which shoes do you need to step to move forward in this area of your life?
   _____
   _____

3. Out of which shoes do you need to step that hold you back?
   _____
   _____

4. What is the one step you can take today to move forward?
   _____
   _____

5. Your life resolution for today:
   "I commit to (action) _____ today, as I move closer to experiencing _____ in my life!"

6. With whom will you share today's life resolution to help hold you accountable?
   _____

EVENING REFLECTION:

Which insights will you take into tomorrow?
_____
_____

Day 203

Throughout our journeys, we can come to love the feeling of loving the feelings within us. We can come to love indulging our senses, rather than starving them. Today, indulge your senses. Love them. Love you!

MORNING REFLECTION: Date: _____

1. What is your reflection from today's quote?

2. Into which shoes do you need to step to move forward in this area of your life?

3. Out of which shoes do you need to step that hold you back?

4. What is the one step you can take today to move forward?

5. Your life resolution for today:
   "I commit to (action) _____ today, as I move closer to experiencing _____ in my life!"

6. With whom will you share today's life resolution to help hold you accountable?

EVENING REFLECTION:

Which insights will you take into tomorrow?

Day 204

Every day, navigating points emerge on your path. They are beacons that draw you closer to where the treasure lies in your life. Today, look and listen for the beacons that will guide you.

MORNING REFLECTION: Date: _____

1. What is your reflection from today's quote?

2. Into which shoes do you need to step to move forward in this area of your life?

3. Out of which shoes do you need to step that hold you back?

4. What is the one step you can take today to move forward?

5. Your life resolution for today:
   "I commit to (action) _____ today, as I move closer to experiencing _____ in my life!"

6. With whom will you share today's life resolution to help hold you accountable?

EVENING REFLECTION:

Which insights will you take into tomorrow?

Day 205

Imagine our lives if every day we woke believing that we had the power to move mountains. Today, awaken your power!

MORNING REFLECTION: Date: _____

1. What is your reflection from today's quote?

2. Into which shoes do you need to step to move forward in this area of your life?

3. Out of which shoes do you need to step that hold you back?

4. What is the one step you can take today to move forward?

5. Your life resolution for today:
   "I commit to (action) _____ today, as I move closer to experiencing _____ in my life!"

6. With whom will you share today's life resolution to help hold you accountable?

EVENING REFLECTION:

Which insights will you take into tomorrow?

Day 206

We can live our biggest and fullest lives, rather than disappearing into a "little life." Today, choose to leap into your biggest life!

MORNING REFLECTION: Date: _____

1. What is your reflection from today's quote?

2. Into which shoes do you need to step to move forward in this area of your life?

3. Out of which shoes do you need to step that hold you back?

4. What is the one step you can take today to move forward?

5. Your life resolution for today:
   "I commit to (action) _____ today, as I move closer to experiencing _____ in my life!"

6. With whom will you share today's life resolution to help hold you accountable?

EVENING REFLECTION:

Which insights will you take into tomorrow?

Day 207

We become empowered when we share our stories. Otherwise, we hold ourselves prisoners in our silence. Today, release yourself from silence!

MORNING REFLECTION: Date: _____

1. What is your reflection from today's quote?
   _____
   _____

2. Into which shoes do you need to step to move forward in this area of your life?
   _____
   _____

3. Out of which shoes do you need to step that hold you back?
   _____
   _____

4. What is the one step you can take today to move forward?
   _____
   _____

5. Your life resolution for today:
   "I commit to (action) _____ today, as I move closer to experiencing _____ in my life!"

6. With whom will you share today's life resolution to help hold you accountable?
   _____

EVENING REFLECTION:

Which insights will you take into tomorrow?
_____
_____

Day 208

Your light is within you, waiting for you to release it.
Today, let your brightness outshine your fear!

## MORNING REFLECTION:	Date: _____

1. What is your reflection from today's quote?
   _____
   _____

2. Into which shoes do you need to step to move forward in this area of your life?
   _____
   _____

3. Out of which shoes do you need to step that hold you back?
   _____
   _____

4. What is the one step you can take today to move forward?
   _____
   _____

5. Your life resolution for today:
   "I commit to (action) _____ today, as I
   move closer to experiencing _____ in my life!"

6. With whom will you share today's life resolution to help hold you accountable?
   _____

EVENING REFLECTION:

Which insights will you take into tomorrow?
_____
_____

Day 209

When we choose a path upon which we find inspiration in each moment, we travel to greater heights. Today, leap onto your most inspired path!

MORNING REFLECTION: Date: _____

1. What is your reflection from today's quote?
   _____
   _____

2. Into which shoes do you need to step to move forward in this area of your life?
   _____
   _____

3. Out of which shoes do you need to step that hold you back?
   _____
   _____

4. What is the one step you can take today to move forward?
   _____
   _____

5. Your life resolution for today:
   "I commit to (action) _____ today, as I move closer to experiencing _____ in my life!"

6. With whom will you share today's life resolution to help hold you accountable?
   _____

EVENING REFLECTION:

Which insights will you take into tomorrow?
_____
_____

Day 210

Your destiny is to live in abundance and well-being. Today, decide to take your destiny into your own hands, and act to bring abundance and well-being into your life.

MORNING REFLECTION: Date: _____

1. What is your reflection from today's quote?

2. Into which shoes do you need to step to move forward in this area of your life?

3. Out of which shoes do you need to step that hold you back?

4. What is the one step you can take today to move forward?

5. Your life resolution for today:
   "I commit to (action) _____ today, as I move closer to experiencing _____ in my life!"

6. With whom will you share today's life resolution to help hold you accountable?

EVENING REFLECTION:

Which insights will you take into tomorrow?

Day 211

Irrespective of the god or gods or divine power in which we believe, we each have a higher path fueled by an infinite source of power. Today, allow that power to take you higher!

MORNING REFLECTION: Date: _____

1. What is your reflection from today's quote?

2. Into which shoes do you need to step to move forward in this area of your life?

3. Out of which shoes do you need to step that hold you back?

4. What is the one step you can take today to move forward?

5. Your life resolution for today:
   "I commit to (action) _____ today, as I move closer to experiencing _____ in my life!"

6. With whom will you share today's life resolution to help hold you accountable?

EVENING REFLECTION:

Which insights will you take into tomorrow?

Day 212

The exhibit of our potential to create a masterpiece through the work of our lives surrounds us every day. Today, breathe in the masterpiece around you and be inspired to create your own!

MORNING REFLECTION: Date: _____

1. What is your reflection from today's quote?
   _____
   _____

2. Into which shoes do you need to step to move forward in this area of your life?
   _____
   _____

3. Out of which shoes do you need to step that hold you back?
   _____
   _____

4. What is the one step you can take today to move forward?
   _____
   _____

5. Your life resolution for today:
   "I commit to (action) _____ today, as I move closer to experiencing _____ in my life!"

6. With whom will you share today's life resolution to help hold you accountable?
   _____

EVENING REFLECTION:

Which insights will you take into tomorrow?
_____
_____

Day 213

Sometimes those around us can see more than we are able to see alone. Today, open yourself to messages from another.

MORNING REFLECTION: Date: _____

1. What is your reflection from today's quote?
   _____
   _____

2. Into which shoes do you need to step to move forward in this area of your life?
   _____
   _____

3. Out of which shoes do you need to step that hold you back?
   _____
   _____

4. What is the one step you can take today to move forward?
   _____
   _____

5. Your life resolution for today:
   "I commit to (action) _____ today, as I move closer to experiencing _____ in my life!"

6. With whom will you share today's life resolution to help hold you accountable?
   _____

EVENING REFLECTION:

Which insights will you take into tomorrow?
_____
_____

Day 214

With every smile we give, with every gesture of help, with every word of encouragement, we light a spark inside another, and inside ourselves, which grows into an eternal flame. Today, light up the world with kindness.

MORNING REFLECTION:　　　　　　　　Date: _____

1. What is your reflection from today's quote?

2. Into which shoes do you need to step to move forward in this area of your life?

3. Out of which shoes do you need to step that hold you back?

4. What is the one step you can take today to move forward?

5. Your life resolution for today:
   "I commit to (action) _____ today, as I move closer to experiencing _____ in my life!"

6. With whom will you share today's life resolution to help hold you accountable?

EVENING REFLECTION:

Which insights will you take into tomorrow?

Day 215

The common pursuit of the human spirit is to set ourselves free from whatever chains are holding us. Today, release your chains. Fly free!

MORNING REFLECTION: Date: _____

1. What is your reflection from today's quote?
   _____
   _____

2. Into which shoes do you need to step to move forward in this area of your life?
   _____
   _____

3. Out of which shoes do you need to step that hold you back?
   _____
   _____

4. What is the one step you can take today to move forward?
   _____
   _____

5. Your life resolution for today:
   "I commit to (action) _____ today, as I move closer to experiencing _____ in my life!"

6. With whom will you share today's life resolution to help hold you accountable?
   _____

EVENING REFLECTION:

Which insights will you take into tomorrow?
_____
_____

Day 216

When we pause quietly, and feel the depths of our soul, then we can feel the angels within and release them to carry us on their wings. Today, allow your angels to carry you to your heights!

MORNING REFLECTION: Date: _____

1. What is your reflection from today's quote?
   _____

2. Into which shoes do you need to step to move forward in this area of your life?
   _____

3. Out of which shoes do you need to step that hold you back?
   _____

4. What is the one step you can take today to move forward?
   _____

5. Your life resolution for today:
   "I commit to (action) _____ today, as I move closer to experiencing _____ in my life!"

6. With whom will you share today's life resolution to help hold you accountable?
   _____

EVENING REFLECTION:

Which insights will you take into tomorrow?
_____

Day 217

The quest to constantly renew oneself in order to evolve is at the heart of all creative endeavors of each artist, sculptor, and architect in every city throughout the history. Today, pursue your most creative endeavors in the city of your soul!

MORNING REFLECTION: Date: _____

1. What is your reflection from today's quote?

2. Into which shoes do you need to step to move forward in this area of your life?

3. Out of which shoes do you need to step that hold you back?

4. What is the one step you can take today to move forward?

5. Your life resolution for today:
   "I commit to (action) _____ today, as I move closer to experiencing _____ in my life!"

6. With whom will you share today's life resolution to help hold you accountable?

EVENING REFLECTION:

Which insights will you take into tomorrow?

Day 218

Each new day brings a new canvas upon which we can create a more distinctive, vibrant, and authentic scene. Today, paint with passion and purpose!

MORNING REFLECTION: Date: _____

1. What is your reflection from today's quote?

2. Into which shoes do you need to step to move forward in this area of your life?

3. Out of which shoes do you need to step that hold you back?

4. What is the one step you can take today to move forward?

5. Your life resolution for today:
   "I commit to (action) _____ today, as I move closer to experiencing _____ in my life!"

6. With whom will you share today's life resolution to help hold you accountable?

EVENING REFLECTION:

Which insights will you take into tomorrow?

Day 219

There is no fear at the depths and at the heights. There are only new discoveries, new mysteries, new perspectives, new truths, and new states of being. Today, venture into your depths and heights.

MORNING REFLECTION: Date: _____

1. What is your reflection from today's quote?

2. Into which shoes do you need to step to move forward in this area of your life?

3. Out of which shoes do you need to step that hold you back?

4. What is the one step you can take today to move forward?

5. Your life resolution for today:
   "I commit to (action) _____ today, as I move closer to experiencing _____ in my life!"

6. With whom will you share today's life resolution to help hold you accountable?

EVENING REFLECTION:

Which insights will you take into tomorrow?

Day 220

Our journeys are only just beginning. In each moment, unimaginable new opportunities emerge. Today, pay attention to the opportunities in the moments!

MORNING REFLECTION: Date: _____

1. What is your reflection from today's quote?

2. Into which shoes do you need to step to move forward in this area of your life?

3. Out of which shoes do you need to step that hold you back?

4. What is the one step you can take today to move forward?

5. Your life resolution for today:
   "I commit to (action) _____ today, as I move closer to experiencing _____ in my life!"

6. With whom will you share today's life resolution to help hold you accountable?

EVENING REFLECTION:

Which insights will you take into tomorrow?

Day 221

The messages that rise from within us are our greatest guides—they come from our divine source. They grow with each conscious breath and each contemplative pause. Today, breathe, pause, listen.

MORNING REFLECTION: Date: _____

1. What is your reflection from today's quote?
   _____
   _____

2. Into which shoes do you need to step to move forward in this area of your life?
   _____
   _____

3. Out of which shoes do you need to step that hold you back?
   _____
   _____

4. What is the one step you can take today to move forward?
   _____
   _____

5. Your life resolution for today:
   "I commit to (action) _____ today, as I move closer to experiencing _____ in my life!"

6. With whom will you share today's life resolution to help hold you accountable?

EVENING REFLECTION:

Which insights will you take into tomorrow?
_____
_____

Day 222

Losing pain is like losing weight—we need to stick with it every day. We need to create a "nutritional emotional diet." We need to fuel ourselves with things that energize us, and eliminate things that are harmful. Today, start losing your pain.

MORNING REFLECTION: Date: _____

1. What is your reflection from today's quote?

2. Into which shoes do you need to step to move forward in this area of your life?

3. Out of which shoes do you need to step that hold you back?

4. What is the one step you can take today to move forward?

5. Your life resolution for today:
   "I commit to (action) _____ today, as I move closer to experiencing _____ in my life!"

6. With whom will you share today's life resolution to help hold you accountable?

EVENING REFLECTION:

Which insights will you take into tomorrow?

Day 223

Often we get stuck in the role of victim and feel at the mercy of all that is around, rather than feel we have the strength to break free. Yet, we have more than the strength to break free—we have the choice. Today, choose your freedom!

MORNING REFLECTION: Date: _____

1. What is your reflection from today's quote?

2. Into which shoes do you need to step to move forward in this area of your life?

3. Out of which shoes do you need to step that hold you back?

4. What is the one step you can take today to move forward?

5. Your life resolution for today:
   "I commit to (action) _____ today, as I move closer to experiencing _____ in my life!"

6. With whom will you share today's life resolution to help hold you accountable?

EVENING REFLECTION:

Which insights will you take into tomorrow?

Day 224

Our greatest adventures lie not outside ourselves, but within ourselves, and one ultimately leads to the other. Today, start an adventure!

MORNING REFLECTION: Date: _____

1. What is your reflection from today's quote?

2. Into which shoes do you need to step to move forward in this area of your life?

3. Out of which shoes do you need to step that hold you back?

4. What is the one step you can take today to move forward?

5. Your life resolution for today:
   "I commit to (action) _____ today, as I move closer to experiencing _____ in my life!"

6. With whom will you share today's life resolution to help hold you accountable?

EVENING REFLECTION:

Which insights will you take into tomorrow?

Day 225

You are the only one who can create your reality. In each moment you can choose to take hold of your journey and step into all you want for your life. Today, embark upon your greatest journey.

MORNING REFLECTION: Date: _____

1. What is your reflection from today's quote?

2. Into which shoes do you need to step to move forward in this area of your life?

3. Out of which shoes do you need to step that hold you back?

4. What is the one step you can take today to move forward?

5. Your life resolution for today:
   "I commit to (action) _____ today, as I move closer to experiencing _____ in my life!"

6. With whom will you share today's life resolution to help hold you accountable?

EVENING REFLECTION:

Which insights will you take into tomorrow?

Day 226

We are each created uniquely with the capacity to experience infinite love and happiness. Today, live infinitely.

MORNING REFLECTION: Date: _____

1. What is your reflection from today's quote?
   _____
   _____

2. Into which shoes do you need to step to move forward in this area of your life?
   _____
   _____

3. Out of which shoes do you need to step that hold you back?
   _____
   _____

4. What is the one step you can take today to move forward?
   _____
   _____

5. Your life resolution for today:
   "I commit to (action) _____ today, as I move closer to experiencing _____ in my life!"

6. With whom will you share today's life resolution to help hold you accountable?
   _____

EVENING REFLECTION:

Which insights will you take into tomorrow?
_____
_____

Day 227

Within the present moment are infinite possibilities to ascend life—to rise above the worst that has happened and live defiantly in your highest purpose. You are here to be great. Today, rise and let no-one hold you down.

MORNING REFLECTION: Date:

1. What is your reflection from today's quote?

2. Into which shoes do you need to step to move forward in this area of your life?

3. Out of which shoes do you need to step that hold you back?

4. What is the one step you can take today to move forward?

5. Your life resolution for today:
   "I commit to (action) _____ today, as I move closer to experiencing _____ in my life!"

6. With whom will you share today's life resolution to help hold you accountable?

EVENING REFLECTION:

Which insights will you take into tomorrow?

Day 228

When we unveil the angels within us, we can transform each moment to help ourselves and to help one another soar to our greatest heights. Today, soar with your angels.

MORNING REFLECTION: Date: _____

1. What is your reflection from today's quote?
   _____
   _____

2. Into which shoes do you need to step to move forward in this area of your life?
   _____

3. Out of which shoes do you need to step that hold you back?
   _____

4. What is the one step you can take today to move forward?
   _____
   _____

5. Your life resolution for today:
   "I commit to (action) _____ today, as I move closer to experiencing _____ in my life!"

6. With whom will you share today's life resolution to help hold you accountable?
   _____

EVENING REFLECTION:

Which insights will you take into tomorrow?
_____
_____

Day 229

We can all live bigger. We can move mountains for ourselves. We can move mountains for others. We simply need to think bigger. Today, think big.

MORNING REFLECTION: Date: _____

1. What is your reflection from today's quote?

2. Into which shoes do you need to step to move forward in this area of your life?

3. Out of which shoes do you need to step that hold you back?

4. What is the one step you can take today to move forward?

5. Your life resolution for today:
   "I commit to (action) _____ today, as I move closer to experiencing _____ in my life!"

6. With whom will you share today's life resolution to help hold you accountable?

EVENING REFLECTION:

Which insights will you take into tomorrow?

Day 230

No matter where you stand today, your life has brought you here for a reason. Today, pause, and listen.

MORNING REFLECTION: Date: _____

1. What is your reflection from today's quote?
   _____
   _____

2. Into which shoes do you need to step to move forward in this area of your life?
   _____
   _____

3. Out of which shoes do you need to step that hold you back?
   _____
   _____

4. What is the one step you can take today to move forward?
   _____
   _____

5. Your life resolution for today:
   "I commit to (action) _____ today, as I move closer to experiencing _____ in my life!"

6. With whom will you share today's life resolution to help hold you accountable?
   _____

EVENING REFLECTION:

Which insights will you take into tomorrow?
_____

Day 231

When we allow ourselves to pause, breathe, and look around us, we will see the magic in the world and in ourselves. Today, let magic come alive in you.

MORNING REFLECTION: Date: _____

1. What is your reflection from today's quote?
   _____
   _____

2. Into which shoes do you need to step to move forward in this area of your life?
   _____
   _____

3. Out of which shoes do you need to step that hold you back?
   _____
   _____

4. What is the one step you can take today to move forward?
   _____
   _____

5. Your life resolution for today:
   "I commit to (action) _____ today, as I move closer to experiencing _____ in my life!"

6. With whom will you share today's life resolution to help hold you accountable?

EVENING REFLECTION:

Which insights will you take into tomorrow?
_____
_____

Day 232

If we want to stand firmly for ourselves, and to reach beyond the things that hold us back, we need to start by giving voice to the things that keep us silent. Today, let your voice be heard!

MORNING REFLECTION: Date: _____

1. What is your reflection from today's quote?

2. Into which shoes do you need to step to move forward in this area of your life?

3. Out of which shoes do you need to step that hold you back?

4. What is the one step you can take today to move forward?

5. Your life resolution for today:
   "I commit to (action) _____ today, as I move closer to experiencing _____ in my life!"

6. With whom will you share today's life resolution to help hold you accountable?

EVENING REFLECTION:

Which insights will you take into tomorrow?

Day 233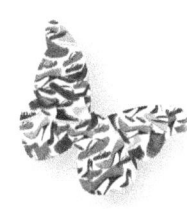

Our challenges may seem insurmountable, yet there is always a way. We just need to have the attitude to reach our highest altitude. Today, have attitude!

MORNING REFLECTION: Date: _____

1. What is your reflection from today's quote?
   _____
   _____

2. Into which shoes do you need to step to move forward in this area of your life?
   _____
   _____

3. Out of which shoes do you need to step that hold you back?
   _____
   _____

4. What is the one step you can take today to move forward?
   _____
   _____

5. Your life resolution for today:
   "I commit to (action) _____ today, as I move closer to experiencing _____ in my life!"

6. With whom will you share today's life resolution to help hold you accountable?
   _____

EVENING REFLECTION:

Which insights will you take into tomorrow?
_____

Day 234

Your feelings, not how others would like you to feel, are your most reliable guide on your journey. Today, listen to your feelings!

MORNING REFLECTION: Date: _____

1. What is your reflection from today's quote?

2. Into which shoes do you need to step to move forward in this area of your life?

3. Out of which shoes do you need to step that hold you back?

4. What is the one step you can take today to move forward?

5. Your life resolution for today:
   "I commit to (action) _____ today, as I move closer to experiencing _____ in my life!"

6. With whom will you share today's life resolution to help hold you accountable?

EVENING REFLECTION:

Which insights will you take into tomorrow?

Day 235

Our words can change our world.
Today, choose your words.

MORNING REFLECTION: Date: _____

1. What is your reflection from today's quote?
   _____
   _____

2. Into which shoes do you need to step to move forward in this area of your life?
   _____
   _____

3. Out of which shoes do you need to step that hold you back?
   _____
   _____

4. What is the one step you can take today to move forward?
   _____
   _____

5. Your life resolution for today:
   "I commit to (action) _____ today, as I move closer to experiencing _____ in my life!"

6. With whom will you share today's life resolution to help hold you accountable?
   _____

EVENING REFLECTION:

Which insights will you take into tomorrow?
_____

Day 236

When you don't give up, you cannot fail.
Today, keep going!

MORNING REFLECTION: Date: _____

1. What is your reflection from today's quote?

2. Into which shoes do you need to step to move forward in this area of your life?

3. Out of which shoes do you need to step that hold you back?

4. What is the one step you can take today to move forward?

5. Your life resolution for today:
   "I commit to (action) _____ today, as I move closer to experiencing _____ in my life!"

6. With whom will you share today's life resolution to help hold you accountable?

EVENING REFLECTION:

Which insights will you take into tomorrow?

Day 237

As you conquer the pieces of your self that don't serve you, you create more space for pieces of your self that are born of your soul to emerge. Today, create space for your soul.

MORNING REFLECTION: Date: _____

1. What is your reflection from today's quote?
   _____
   _____

2. Into which shoes do you need to step to move forward in this area of your life?
   _____
   _____

3. Out of which shoes do you need to step that hold you back?
   _____
   _____

4. What is the one step you can take today to move forward?
   _____
   _____

5. Your life resolution for today:
   "I commit to (action) _____ today, as I move closer to experiencing _____ in my life!"

6. With whom will you share today's life resolution to help hold you accountable?

EVENING REFLECTION:

Which insights will you take into tomorrow?
_____
_____

Day 238

You can pause and hear the music of your soul rising through the thunderstorms of your shattered pieces. Today, hear the music within you!

MORNING REFLECTION: Date: _____

1. What is your reflection from today's quote?

2. Into which shoes do you need to step to move forward in this area of your life?

3. Out of which shoes do you need to step that hold you back?

4. What is the one step you can take today to move forward?

5. Your life resolution for today:
   "I commit to (action) _____ today, as I move closer to experiencing _____ in my life!"

6. With whom will you share today's life resolution to help hold you accountable?

EVENING REFLECTION:

Which insights will you take into tomorrow?

Day 239

People come into our lives for a reason.
Today, see beyond the person to the reason.

MORNING REFLECTION: Date: _____

1. What is your reflection from today's quote?
   _____
   _____

2. Into which shoes do you need to step to move forward in this area of your life?
   _____
   _____

3. Out of which shoes do you need to step that hold you back?
   _____
   _____

4. What is the one step you can take today to move forward?
   _____
   _____

5. Your life resolution for today:
   "I commit to (action) _____ today, as I
   move closer to experiencing _____ in my life!"

6. With whom will you share today's life resolution to help hold you accountable?

EVENING REFLECTION:

Which insights will you take into tomorrow?
_____
_____

Day 240

Before we can heal, we need to feel there is something worth healing for. Today, find worth.

MORNING REFLECTION: Date: _____

1. What is your reflection from today's quote?
   _____
   _____

2. Into which shoes do you need to step to move forward in this area of your life?
   _____
   _____

3. Out of which shoes do you need to step that hold you back?
   _____
   _____

4. What is the one step you can take today to move forward?
   _____
   _____

5. Your life resolution for today:
   "I commit to (action) _____ today, as I move closer to experiencing _____ in my life!"

6. With whom will you share today's life resolution to help hold you accountable?
   _____

EVENING REFLECTION:

Which insights will you take into tomorrow?
_____
_____

Day 241

In each moment, we can breathe in and ignite the light within us, we can feel the infinite possibilities of the universe fill our consciousness. Today, feel the breath of your infinite possibilities.

MORNING REFLECTION: Date: _____

1. What is your reflection from today's quote?
   _____

2. Into which shoes do you need to step to move forward in this area of your life?
   _____

3. Out of which shoes do you need to step that hold you back?
   _____

4. What is the one step you can take today to move forward?
   _____

5. Your life resolution for today:
   "I commit to (action) _____ today, as I move closer to experiencing _____ in my life!"

6. With whom will you share today's life resolution to help hold you accountable?
   _____

EVENING REFLECTION:

Which insights will you take into tomorrow?
_____

Day 242

Through my journey, the universe showed me that greener grass existed. I saw life and laughter. There was a point to existing. There was a life worth living. There was a life worth loving. Today, let the universe show you greener grass.

MORNING REFLECTION: Date: _____

1. What is your reflection from today's quote?

2. Into which shoes do you need to step to move forward in this area of your life?

3. Out of which shoes do you need to step that hold you back?

4. What is the one step you can take today to move forward?

5. Your life resolution for today:
   "I commit to (action) _____ today, as I move closer to experiencing _____ in my life!"

6. With whom will you share today's life resolution to help hold you accountable?

EVENING REFLECTION:

Which insights will you take into tomorrow?

Day 243

We are all children of the universe, and if we are not here for each other, then one wonders why there are so many of us sharing this one space. Today, be for another.

MORNING REFLECTION: Date: _____

1. What is your reflection from today's quote?
   _____
   _____

2. Into which shoes do you need to step to move forward in this area of your life?
   _____
   _____

3. Out of which shoes do you need to step that hold you back?
   _____
   _____

4. What is the one step you can take today to move forward?
   _____
   _____

5. Your life resolution for today:
   "I commit to (action) _____ today, as I move closer to experiencing _____ in my life!"

6. With whom will you share today's life resolution to help hold you accountable?
   _____

EVENING REFLECTION:

Which insights will you take into tomorrow?
_____
_____

Day 244

In this present moment we are the sum of all that we choose to be. Today, choose to be your greatest!

MORNING REFLECTION: Date: _____

1. What is your reflection from today's quote?

2. Into which shoes do you need to step to move forward in this area of your life?

3. Out of which shoes do you need to step that hold you back?

4. What is the one step you can take today to move forward?

5. Your life resolution for today:
   "I commit to (action) _____ today, as I move closer to experiencing _____ in my life!"

6. With whom will you share today's life resolution to help hold you accountable?

EVENING REFLECTION:

Which insights will you take into tomorrow?

Day 245

When we compromise the love we give and accept, our lives becomes like faded pieces of art. Today, restore the masterpiece of your life with vibrant, uncompromising love.

MORNING REFLECTION: Date: _____

1. What is your reflection from today's quote?
   _____
   _____

2. Into which shoes do you need to step to move forward in this area of your life?
   _____
   _____

3. Out of which shoes do you need to step that hold you back?
   _____
   _____

4. What is the one step you can take today to move forward?
   _____
   _____

5. Your life resolution for today:
   "I commit to (action) _____ today, as I move closer to experiencing _____ in my life!"

6. With whom will you share today's life resolution to help hold you accountable?
   _____

EVENING REFLECTION:

Which insights will you take into tomorrow?
_____

Day 246

In your darkest times, have faith that the forces of light that illuminate your truths, your dreams, and your soul, are so much more powerful than any of the forces of darkness. Today, live in light.

MORNING REFLECTION: Date: _____

1. What is your reflection from today's quote?
   _____
   _____

2. Into which shoes do you need to step to move forward in this area of your life?
   _____
   _____

3. Out of which shoes do you need to step that hold you back?
   _____
   _____

4. What is the one step you can take today to move forward?
   _____
   _____

5. Your life resolution for today:
   "I commit to (action) _____ today, as I move closer to experiencing _____ in my life!"

6. With whom will you share today's life resolution to help hold you accountable?
   _____

EVENING REFLECTION:

Which insights will you take into tomorrow?
_____
_____

Day 247

If we are not brave enough to travel to the deepest and darkest parts of ourselves, we can never be daring enough to take ourselves to our greatest heights. Today, travel deep, fly high.

MORNING REFLECTION: Date:

1. What is your reflection from today's quote?

2. Into which shoes do you need to step to move forward in this area of your life?

3. Out of which shoes do you need to step that hold you back?

4. What is the one step you can take today to move forward?

5. Your life resolution for today:
   "I commit to (action) _____ today, as I move closer to experiencing _____ in my life!"

6. With whom will you share today's life resolution to help hold you accountable?

EVENING REFLECTION:

Which insights will you take into tomorrow?

Day 248

We are part of an extraordinary state of being with the universe, with so much magical potential. Today, reveal the magic within you.

MORNING REFLECTION: Date: _____

1. What is your reflection from today's quote?
   _____

2. Into which shoes do you need to step to move forward in this area of your life?
   _____

3. Out of which shoes do you need to step that hold you back?
   _____

4. What is the one step you can take today to move forward?
   _____

5. Your life resolution for today:
   "I commit to (action) _____ today, as I move closer to experiencing _____ in my life!"

6. With whom will you share today's life resolution to help hold you accountable?
   _____

EVENING REFLECTION:

Which insights will you take into tomorrow?
_____

Day 249

The journeys that you set upon to uncover your soul do not need to be journeys to far away places. Your soul is closer to you than any place to which you can travel. Today, journey within.

MORNING REFLECTION: Date: _____

1. What is your reflection from today's quote?
   _____
   _____

2. Into which shoes do you need to step to move forward in this area of your life?
   _____
   _____

3. Out of which shoes do you need to step that hold you back?
   _____
   _____

4. What is the one step you can take today to move forward?
   _____
   _____

5. Your life resolution for today:
   "I commit to (action) _____ today, as I move closer to experiencing _____ in my life!"

6. With whom will you share today's life resolution to help hold you accountable?
   _____

EVENING REFLECTION:

Which insights will you take into tomorrow?
_____
_____

Day 250

In life, in order to transition, we must step across the bridges. If not, we simply remain, wondering what might lie beyond, and then turn to retrace old paths. Today, cross bridges.

MORNING REFLECTION: Date: _____

1. What is your reflection from today's quote?
   _____
   _____

2. Into which shoes do you need to step to move forward in this area of your life?
   _____
   _____

3. Out of which shoes do you need to step that hold you back?
   _____
   _____

4. What is the one step you can take today to move forward?
   _____
   _____

5. Your life resolution for today:
   "I commit to (action) _____ today, as I move closer to experiencing _____ in my life!"

6. With whom will you share today's life resolution to help hold you accountable?
   _____

EVENING REFLECTION:

Which insights will you take into tomorrow?
_____
_____

Day 251

*In your moments of pause, you can see the angel
in the marble of your being and sculpt it until it is free.
Today, sculpt the angel of your being.*

MORNING REFLECTION: Date: _____

1. What is your reflection from today's quote?
   _____
   _____

2. Into which shoes do you need to step to move forward in this area of your life?
   _____
   _____

3. Out of which shoes do you need to step that hold you back?
   _____
   _____

4. What is the one step you can take today to move forward?
   _____
   _____

5. Your life resolution for today:
   "I commit to (action) _____ today, as I
   move closer to experiencing _____ in my life!"

6. With whom will you share today's life resolution to help hold you accountable?
   _____

EVENING REFLECTION:

Which insights will you take into tomorrow?
_____
_____

Day 252

Our physical bodies are infinite vessels of energy. In that field of energy, we are connected to every wisdom of existence. Today, exist in the field of your infinite wisdom.

MORNING REFLECTION: Date: _____

1. What is your reflection from today's quote?
   _____
   _____

2. Into which shoes do you need to step to move forward in this area of your life?
   _____
   _____

3. Out of which shoes do you need to step that hold you back?
   _____
   _____

4. What is the one step you can take today to move forward?
   _____
   _____

5. Your life resolution for today:
   "I commit to (action) _____ today, as I move closer to experiencing _____ in my life!"

6. With whom will you share today's life resolution to help hold you accountable?
   _____

EVENING REFLECTION:

Which insights will you take into tomorrow?
   _____
   _____

Day 253

We often want to help another, yet finding the way can be difficult. Today, find ways.

MORNING REFLECTION: Date: _____

1. What is your reflection from today's quote?
   _____
   _____

2. Into which shoes do you need to step to move forward in this area of your life?
   _____
   _____

3. Out of which shoes do you need to step that hold you back?
   _____
   _____

4. What is the one step you can take today to move forward?
   _____
   _____

5. Your life resolution for today:
   "I commit to (action) _____ today, as I move closer to experiencing _____ in my life!"

6. With whom will you share today's life resolution to help hold you accountable?
   _____

EVENING REFLECTION:

Which insights will you take into tomorrow?
_____
_____

Day 254

In each moment, unimaginable new opportunities emerge.
Today, pause in the moment and discover infinite possibilities.

MORNING REFLECTION: Date: _____

1. What is your reflection from today's quote?

2. Into which shoes do you need to step to move forward in this area of your life?

3. Out of which shoes do you need to step that hold you back?

4. What is the one step you can take today to move forward?

5. Your life resolution for today:
   "I commit to (action) _____ today, as I move closer to experiencing _____ in my life!"

6. With whom will you share today's life resolution to help hold you accountable?

EVENING REFLECTION:

Which insights will you take into tomorrow?

Day 255

Life gives us breath to live in every moment.
Today, breathe the moment fully.

MORNING REFLECTION: Date: _____

1. What is your reflection from today's quote?
   _____
   _____

2. Into which shoes do you need to step to move forward in this area of your life?
   _____
   _____

3. Out of which shoes do you need to step that hold you back?
   _____
   _____

4. What is the one step you can take today to move forward?
   _____
   _____

5. Your life resolution for today:
   "I commit to (action) _____ today, as I
   move closer to experiencing _____ in my life!"

6. With whom will you share today's life resolution to help hold you accountable?
   _____

EVENING REFLECTION:

Which insights will you take into tomorrow?
_____
_____

Day 256

We are the only ones who can give up on ourselves, despite everything that may happen to us—no matter how many people will try to stop us in life. Today, allow no-one to stop you!

MORNING REFLECTION: Date: _____

1. What is your reflection from today's quote?
   _____
   _____

2. Into which shoes do you need to step to move forward in this area of your life?
   _____
   _____

3. Out of which shoes do you need to step that hold you back?
   _____
   _____

4. What is the one step you can take today to move forward?
   _____
   _____

5. Your life resolution for today:
   "I commit to (action) _____ today, as I move closer to experiencing _____ in my life!"

6. With whom will you share today's life resolution to help hold you accountable?
   _____

EVENING REFLECTION:

Which insights will you take into tomorrow?
_____
_____

Day 257

The only way to create a peaceful ebb and flow in the
world around, is to calm the waters in our worlds within.
Today, pause and allow calm to flow through you.

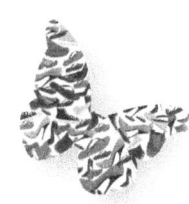

MORNING REFLECTION: Date:

1. What is your reflection from today's quote?

2. Into which shoes do you need to step to move forward in this area of your life?

3. Out of which shoes do you need to step that hold you back?

4. What is the one step you can take today to move forward?

5. Your life resolution for today:
   "I commit to (action) _____ today, as I move closer to experiencing _____ in my life!"

6. With whom will you share today's life resolution to help hold you accountable?

EVENING REFLECTION:

Which insights will you take into tomorrow?

Day 258

All that we need is present in every moment. We simply need to pause, and tap into the limitless potential within us. Today, tap into your limitless self.

MORNING REFLECTION: Date: _____

1. What is your reflection from today's quote?
   _____
   _____

2. Into which shoes do you need to step to move forward in this area of your life?
   _____
   _____

3. Out of which shoes do you need to step that hold you back?
   _____
   _____

4. What is the one step you can take today to move forward?
   _____
   _____

5. Your life resolution for today:
   "I commit to (action) _____ today, as I move closer to experiencing _____ in my life!"

6. With whom will you share today's life resolution to help hold you accountable?
   _____

EVENING REFLECTION:

Which insights will you take into tomorrow?
_____
_____

Day 259

Each day, we can walk hand in hand with the universe, intimately connected to the higher powers that flow through us. Today, walk with the universe.

MORNING REFLECTION: Date: _____

1. What is your reflection from today's quote?
   _____
   _____

2. Into which shoes do you need to step to move forward in this area of your life?
   _____
   _____

3. Out of which shoes do you need to step that hold you back?
   _____
   _____

4. What is the one step you can take today to move forward?
   _____
   _____

5. Your life resolution for today:
   "I commit to (action) _____ today, as I move closer to experiencing _____ in my life!"

6. With whom will you share today's life resolution to help hold you accountable?
   _____

EVENING REFLECTION:

Which insights will you take into tomorrow?
_____

Day 260

Our dreams come within reach as we help others make their dreams become reality. Today, make dreams come true!

MORNING REFLECTION: Date: _____

1. What is your reflection from today's quote?

2. Into which shoes do you need to step to move forward in this area of your life?

3. Out of which shoes do you need to step that hold you back?

4. What is the one step you can take today to move forward?

5. Your life resolution for today:
   "I commit to (action) _____ today, as I move closer to experiencing _____ in my life!"

6. With whom will you share today's life resolution to help hold you accountable?

EVENING REFLECTION:

Which insights will you take into tomorrow?

Day 261

We need to take hold of all of the wonderful pieces of our lives and shape ourselves in the likeness of our greatest dreams and aspirations. Today, take hold of your life, and shape it into your masterpiece!

MORNING REFLECTION: Date: _____

1. What is your reflection from today's quote?
   _____
   _____

2. Into which shoes do you need to step to move forward in this area of your life?
   _____
   _____

3. Out of which shoes do you need to step that hold you back?
   _____
   _____

4. What is the one step you can take today to move forward?
   _____
   _____

5. Your life resolution for today:
   "I commit to (action) _____ today, as I move closer to experiencing _____ in my life!"

6. With whom will you share today's life resolution to help hold you accountable?
   _____

EVENING REFLECTION:

Which insights will you take into tomorrow?
_____

Day 262

When we choose to love fully, we choose to live fully. Today, love and live to your fullest!

MORNING REFLECTION: Date: _____

1. What is your reflection from today's quote?

2. Into which shoes do you need to step to move forward in this area of your life?

3. Out of which shoes do you need to step that hold you back?

4. What is the one step you can take today to move forward?

5. Your life resolution for today:
   "I commit to (action) _____ today, as I move closer to experiencing _____ in my life!"

6. With whom will you share today's life resolution to help hold you accountable?

EVENING REFLECTION:

Which insights will you take into tomorrow?

Day 263

On the steps of discovery, if we stand dormant, we miss the beauty and magic of all that lies beyond. Today, step forward into discovery!

MORNING REFLECTION: Date: _____

1. What is your reflection from today's quote?

2. Into which shoes do you need to step to move forward in this area of your life?

3. Out of which shoes do you need to step that hold you back?

4. What is the one step you can take today to move forward?

5. Your life resolution for today:
   "I commit to (action) _____ today, as I move closer to experiencing _____ in my life!"

6. With whom will you share today's life resolution to help hold you accountable?

EVENING REFLECTION:

Which insights will you take into tomorrow?

Day 264

You can soar to your greatest self on the wings of your soul. Today, spread your wings!

MORNING REFLECTION: Date: _____

1. What is your reflection from today's quote?

2. Into which shoes do you need to step to move forward in this area of your life?

3. Out of which shoes do you need to step that hold you back?

4. What is the one step you can take today to move forward?

5. Your life resolution for today:
   "I commit to (action) _____ today, as I move closer to experiencing _____ in my life!"

6. With whom will you share today's life resolution to help hold you accountable?

EVENING REFLECTION:

Which insights will you take into tomorrow?

Day 265

Don't let the world around get you down.
Today, reach within and play in the joy of your soul.

MORNING REFLECTION: Date: _____

1. What is your reflection from today's quote?
   _____
   _____

2. Into which shoes do you need to step to move forward in this area of your life?
   _____
   _____

3. Out of which shoes do you need to step that hold you back?
   _____
   _____

4. What is the one step you can take today to move forward?
   _____
   _____

5. Your life resolution for today:
   "I commit to (action) _____ today, as I move closer to experiencing _____ in my life!"

6. With whom will you share today's life resolution to help hold you accountable?
   _____

EVENING REFLECTION:

Which insights will you take into tomorrow?
   _____
   _____

Day 266

In every moment we can turn the key to release happiness into our lives, and to allow healing waters to flow through us. Today, turn the key to release your happiness.

MORNING REFLECTION: Date: _____

1. What is your reflection from today's quote?
   _____
   _____

2. Into which shoes do you need to step to move forward in this area of your life?
   _____
   _____

3. Out of which shoes do you need to step that hold you back?
   _____
   _____

4. What is the one step you can take today to move forward?
   _____
   _____

5. Your life resolution for today:
   "I commit to (action) _____ today, as I move closer to experiencing _____ in my life!"

6. With whom will you share today's life resolution to help hold you accountable?
   _____

EVENING REFLECTION:

Which insights will you take into tomorrow?
_____
_____

Day 267

We are all children of the universe, set down in our time, with the past as our backdrop and the future as our canvas. Today, imagine your greatest future, and start painting it!

MORNING REFLECTION: Date: _____

1. What is your reflection from today's quote?

2. Into which shoes do you need to step to move forward in this area of your life?

3. Out of which shoes do you need to step that hold you back?

4. What is the one step you can take today to move forward?

5. Your life resolution for today:
   "I commit to (action) _____ today, as I move closer to experiencing _____ in my life!"

6. With whom will you share today's life resolution to help hold you accountable?

EVENING REFLECTION:

Which insights will you take into tomorrow?

Day 268

Our stories can help us step into the shoes of others, and better understand where we stand in our own shoes. Today, consider the question "What is your story?"

MORNING REFLECTION: Date: _____

1. What is your reflection from today's quote?

2. Into which shoes do you need to step to move forward in this area of your life?

3. Out of which shoes do you need to step that hold you back?

4. What is the one step you can take today to move forward?

5. Your life resolution for today:
   "I commit to (action) _____ today, as I move closer to experiencing _____ in my life!"

6. With whom will you share today's life resolution to help hold you accountable?

EVENING REFLECTION:

Which insights will you take into tomorrow?

Day 269

Every stage upon which we stand provides us with the opportunity to "make it." It's up to us to stand upon our stage. To find the courage. To overcome the fear. Today, leap upon your stage!

MORNING REFLECTION: Date: _____

1. What is your reflection from today's quote?
   _____
   _____

2. Into which shoes do you need to step to move forward in this area of your life?
   _____
   _____

3. Out of which shoes do you need to step that hold you back?
   _____
   _____

4. What is the one step you can take today to move forward?
   _____
   _____

5. Your life resolution for today:
   "I commit to (action) _____ today, as I move closer to experiencing _____ in my life!"

6. With whom will you share today's life resolution to help hold you accountable?

EVENING REFLECTION:

Which insights will you take into tomorrow?
_____
_____

Day 270

With every smile that is returned to us, we realize that one person at a time, one smile at a time, we can lighten the load of another. Today, lighten a load!

MORNING REFLECTION: Date: _____

1. What is your reflection from today's quote?
   _____
   _____

2. Into which shoes do you need to step to move forward in this area of your life?
   _____
   _____

3. Out of which shoes do you need to step that hold you back?
   _____
   _____

4. What is the one step you can take today to move forward?
   _____
   _____

5. Your life resolution for today:
   "I commit to (action) _____ today, as I move closer to experiencing _____ in my life!"

6. With whom will you share today's life resolution to help hold you accountable?
   _____

EVENING REFLECTION:

Which insights will you take into tomorrow?
_____
_____

Day 271

With our conscious choices we can create timeless monuments of beauty or lifeless ruins of rubble. Today, make monumental choices!

MORNING REFLECTION: Date: _____

1. What is your reflection from today's quote?

2. Into which shoes do you need to step to move forward in this area of your life?

3. Out of which shoes do you need to step that hold you back?

4. What is the one step you can take today to move forward?

5. Your life resolution for today:
   "I commit to (action) _____ today, as I move closer to experiencing _____ in my life!"

6. With whom will you share today's life resolution to help hold you accountable?

EVENING REFLECTION:

Which insights will you take into tomorrow?

Day 272

We are only limited by our most creative thoughts of what our lives can be. Today, think your most creative thoughts!

MORNING REFLECTION: Date: _____

1. What is your reflection from today's quote?

2. Into which shoes do you need to step to move forward in this area of your life?

3. Out of which shoes do you need to step that hold you back?

4. What is the one step you can take today to move forward?

5. Your life resolution for today:
   "I commit to (action) _____ today, as I move closer to experiencing _____ in my life!"

6. With whom will you share today's life resolution to help hold you accountable?

EVENING REFLECTION:

Which insights will you take into tomorrow?

Day 273

In each moment, we have the choice to reach to greater places.
Today, reach beyond the ordinary, and be extraordinary!

MORNING REFLECTION: Date: _____

1. What is your reflection from today's quote?
   _____
   _____

2. Into which shoes do you need to step to move forward in this area of your life?
   _____
   _____

3. Out of which shoes do you need to step that hold you back?
   _____
   _____

4. What is the one step you can take today to move forward?
   _____
   _____

5. Your life resolution for today:
   "I commit to (action) _____ today, as I
   move closer to experiencing _____ in my life!"

6. With whom will you share today's life resolution to help hold you accountable?
   _____

EVENING REFLECTION:

Which insights will you take into tomorrow?
_____
_____

Day 274

With each step we take, with every choice we make to keep going, we move further away from all that holds us back. Our fears fade, and there is nothing we cannot do. Today, step out of your fears.

MORNING REFLECTION: Date: _____

1. What is your reflection from today's quote?
   _____
   _____

2. Into which shoes do you need to step to move forward in this area of your life?
   _____
   _____

3. Out of which shoes do you need to step that hold you back?
   _____
   _____

4. What is the one step you can take today to move forward?
   _____
   _____

5. Your life resolution for today:
   "I commit to (action) _____ today, as I move closer to experiencing _____ in my life!"

6. With whom will you share today's life resolution to help hold you accountable?
   _____

EVENING REFLECTION:

Which insights will you take into tomorrow?
_____
_____

Day 275

As our sense of purpose in life grows,
so too does the feeling of being at home in life.
Today, find purpose. Find home.

MORNING REFLECTION: Date: _____

1. What is your reflection from today's quote?
   _____
   _____

2. Into which shoes do you need to step to move forward in this area of your life?
   _____
   _____

3. Out of which shoes do you need to step that hold you back?
   _____
   _____

4. What is the one step you can take today to move forward?
   _____
   _____

5. Your life resolution for today:
   "I commit to (action) _____ today, as I
   move closer to experiencing _____ in my life!"

6. With whom will you share today's life resolution to help hold you accountable?
   _____

EVENING REFLECTION:

Which insights will you take into tomorrow?
_____
_____

Day 276

As a young adult, I thought that helping myself was enough to live. Now, I know that I can live bigger by helping others. Today, live your biggest!

MORNING REFLECTION: Date:

1. What is your reflection from today's quote?

2. Into which shoes do you need to step to move forward in this area of your life?

3. Out of which shoes do you need to step that hold you back?

4. What is the one step you can take today to move forward?

5. Your life resolution for today:
   "I commit to (action) _____ today, as I move closer to experiencing _____ in my life!"

6. With whom will you share today's life resolution to help hold you accountable?

EVENING REFLECTION:

Which insights will you take into tomorrow?

Day 277

When so much is stripped from us, there is so much space to refill. Today, see your empty spaces as gift boxes ready to be filled, and fill them!

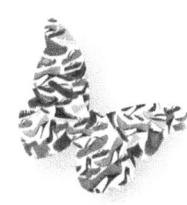

MORNING REFLECTION: Date: _____

1. What is your reflection from today's quote?

2. Into which shoes do you need to step to move forward in this area of your life?

3. Out of which shoes do you need to step that hold you back?

4. What is the one step you can take today to move forward?

5. Your life resolution for today:
   "I commit to (action) _____ today, as I move closer to experiencing _____ in my life!"

6. With whom will you share today's life resolution to help hold you accountable?

EVENING REFLECTION:

Which insights will you take into tomorrow?

Day 278

If no-one else praises you, praise yourself.
You are the voice of the universe, and there is no
greater source of praise. Today, praise you!

MORNING REFLECTION: Date: _____

1. What is your reflection from today's quote?
   _____
   _____

2. Into which shoes do you need to step to move forward in this area of your life?
   _____
   _____

3. Out of which shoes do you need to step that hold you back?
   _____
   _____

4. What is the one step you can take today to move forward?
   _____
   _____

5. Your life resolution for today:
   "I commit to (action) _____ today, as I
   move closer to experiencing _____ in my life!"

6. With whom will you share today's life resolution to help hold you accountable?
   _____

EVENING REFLECTION:

Which insights will you take into tomorrow?
_____
_____

Day 279

Our choices in each moment determine how far and how quickly we reach our greatest potential. Today, make choices that take you farther and higher!

MORNING REFLECTION: Date: _____

1. What is your reflection from today's quote?
   _____
   _____

2. Into which shoes do you need to step to move forward in this area of your life?
   _____
   _____

3. Out of which shoes do you need to step that hold you back?
   _____
   _____

4. What is the one step you can take today to move forward?
   _____
   _____

5. Your life resolution for today:
   "I commit to (action) _____ today, as I move closer to experiencing _____ in my life!"

6. With whom will you share today's life resolution to help hold you accountable?
   _____

EVENING REFLECTION:

Which insights will you take into tomorrow?
_____
_____

Day 280

As a child, I didn't know I had power and I became a victim. As an adult, I have grown to experience authentic power, and I choose to live in that power. Today, live in your authentic power!

MORNING REFLECTION: Date: _____

1. What is your reflection from today's quote?

2. Into which shoes do you need to step to move forward in this area of your life?

3. Out of which shoes do you need to step that hold you back?

4. What is the one step you can take today to move forward?

5. Your life resolution for today:
   "I commit to (action) _____ today, as I move closer to experiencing _____ in my life!"

6. With whom will you share today's life resolution to help hold you accountable?

EVENING REFLECTION:

Which insights will you take into tomorrow?

Day 281

To touch your soul is to ignite your most powerful presence. Today, touch your soul!

MORNING REFLECTION: Date: _____

1. What is your reflection from today's quote?
   _____
   _____

2. Into which shoes do you need to step to move forward in this area of your life?
   _____
   _____

3. Out of which shoes do you need to step that hold you back?
   _____
   _____

4. What is the one step you can take today to move forward?
   _____
   _____

5. Your life resolution for today:
   "I commit to (action) _____ today, as I move closer to experiencing _____ in my life!"

6. With whom will you share today's life resolution to help hold you accountable?
   _____

EVENING REFLECTION:

Which insights will you take into tomorrow?
_____
_____

Day 282

In this moment, you can choose how to use your presence to touch your life and the lives of others to become your most purposeful self. Today, step forward with your greatest presence.

MORNING REFLECTION: Date: _____

1. What is your reflection from today's quote?
   _____
   _____

2. Into which shoes do you need to step to move forward in this area of your life?
   _____
   _____

3. Out of which shoes do you need to step that hold you back?
   _____
   _____

4. What is the one step you can take today to move forward?
   _____
   _____

5. Your life resolution for today:
   "I commit to (action) _____ today, as I move closer to experiencing _____ in my life!"

6. With whom will you share today's life resolution to help hold you accountable?
   _____

EVENING REFLECTION:

Which insights will you take into tomorrow?
_____
_____

Day 283

We have so much to learn from the journeys of each other. We just need to pause to hear. We have so much in common with each other. We just need to pause to see. Today, pause to experience another!

MORNING REFLECTION: Date: _____

1. What is your reflection from today's quote?
   _____
   _____

2. Into which shoes do you need to step to move forward in this area of your life?
   _____
   _____

3. Out of which shoes do you need to step that hold you back?
   _____
   _____

4. What is the one step you can take today to move forward?
   _____
   _____

5. Your life resolution for today:
   "I commit to (action) _____ today, as I move closer to experiencing _____ in my life!"

6. With whom will you share today's life resolution to help hold you accountable?
   _____

EVENING REFLECTION:

Which insights will you take into tomorrow?
_____
_____

Day 284

Without plunging into the depths of your self, the heights to which you can soar will always be limited. Today, plunge into your depths!

MORNING REFLECTION: Date: _____

1. What is your reflection from today's quote?

2. Into which shoes do you need to step to move forward in this area of your life?

3. Out of which shoes do you need to step that hold you back?

4. What is the one step you can take today to move forward?

5. Your life resolution for today:
   "I commit to (action) _____ today, as I move closer to experiencing _____ in my life!"

6. With whom will you share today's life resolution to help hold you accountable?

EVENING REFLECTION:

Which insights will you take into tomorrow?

Day 285

The opportunity for balance and harmony, for calm after the storm, for emerging from our darkest places and stepping into the sunshine, is there for each of us, wherever we are. Today, step into the sunshine!

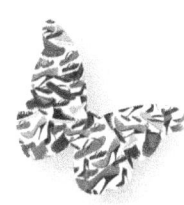

MORNING REFLECTION: Date: _____

1. What is your reflection from today's quote?
   _____
   _____

2. Into which shoes do you need to step to move forward in this area of your life?
   _____
   _____

3. Out of which shoes do you need to step that hold you back?
   _____
   _____

4. What is the one step you can take today to move forward?
   _____
   _____

5. Your life resolution for today:
   "I commit to (action) _____ today, as I move closer to experiencing _____ in my life!"

6. With whom will you share today's life resolution to help hold you accountable?
   _____

EVENING REFLECTION:

Which insights will you take into tomorrow?
_____
_____

Day 286

We don't know what will unfold on the paths ahead, yet if we pause long enough we can feel what feels right and what feels wrong. Today, pause and feel.

MORNING REFLECTION: Date: _____

1. What is your reflection from today's quote?
   _____

2. Into which shoes do you need to step to move forward in this area of your life?
   _____

3. Out of which shoes do you need to step that hold you back?
   _____

4. What is the one step you can take today to move forward?
   _____

5. Your life resolution for today:
   "I commit to (action) _____ today, as I move closer to experiencing _____ in my life!"

6. With whom will you share today's life resolution to help hold you accountable?
   _____

EVENING REFLECTION:

Which insights will you take into tomorrow?
_____

Day 287

Within each first step, there is always doubt and fear, yet if we let the sense of freedom and opportunity overcome the fear, all else will follow. Today, take the first step!

MORNING REFLECTION: Date: _____

1. What is your reflection from today's quote?

2. Into which shoes do you need to step to move forward in this area of your life?

3. Out of which shoes do you need to step that hold you back?

4. What is the one step you can take today to move forward?

5. Your life resolution for today:
   "I commit to (action) _____ today, as I move closer to experiencing _____ in my life!"

6. With whom will you share today's life resolution to help hold you accountable?

EVENING REFLECTION:

Which insights will you take into tomorrow?

Day 288

We must be brave and courageous—for the sake of our own lives, for the sake of the love we desire, and for the sake of our freedom in this one short and precious life. Today, be brave! Be courageous!

MORNING REFLECTION: Date: _____

1. What is your reflection from today's quote?
   _____
   _____

2. Into which shoes do you need to step to move forward in this area of your life?
   _____

3. Out of which shoes do you need to step that hold you back?
   _____

4. What is the one step you can take today to move forward?
   _____

5. Your life resolution for today:
   "I commit to (action) _____ today, as I move closer to experiencing _____ in my life!"

6. With whom will you share today's life resolution to help hold you accountable?
   _____

EVENING REFLECTION:

Which insights will you take into tomorrow?
_____
_____

Day 289

You are the painter of the canvas of your life. Why would you choose to settle for anything less than creating the most wonderful, vibrant, inspiring masterpiece? Today, paint your most inspiring canvas!

MORNING REFLECTION: Date:

1. What is your reflection from today's quote?

2. Into which shoes do you need to step to move forward in this area of your life?

3. Out of which shoes do you need to step that hold you back?

4. What is the one step you can take today to move forward?

5. Your life resolution for today:
   "I commit to (action) _____ today, as I move closer to experiencing _____ in my life!"

6. With whom will you share today's life resolution to help hold you accountable?

EVENING REFLECTION:

Which insights will you take into tomorrow?

Day 290

When we allow purpose to guide our lives, we start to feel more at home in life. Today, find home.

MORNING REFLECTION: Date: _____

1. What is your reflection from today's quote?
   _____
   _____

2. Into which shoes do you need to step to move forward in this area of your life?
   _____
   _____

3. Out of which shoes do you need to step that hold you back?
   _____
   _____

4. What is the one step you can take today to move forward?
   _____
   _____

5. Your life resolution for today:
   "I commit to (action) _____ today, as I move closer to experiencing _____ in my life!"

6. With whom will you share today's life resolution to help hold you accountable?
   _____

EVENING REFLECTION:

Which insights will you take into tomorrow?
_____
_____

Day 291

We are each other's teachers and students.
Today, teach and learn!

MORNING REFLECTION: Date: _____

1. What is your reflection from today's quote?
   _____
   _____

2. Into which shoes do you need to step to move forward in this area of your life?
   _____
   _____

3. Out of which shoes do you need to step that hold you back?
   _____
   _____

4. What is the one step you can take today to move forward?
   _____
   _____

5. Your life resolution for today:
   "I commit to (action) _____ today, as I
   move closer to experiencing _____ in my life!"

6. With whom will you share today's life resolution to help hold you accountable?
   _____

EVENING REFLECTION:

Which insights will you take into tomorrow?
_____
_____

Day 292

Love your family, love yourself, love strangers.
Today, love yourself first.

MORNING REFLECTION: Date: _____

1. What is your reflection from today's quote?
   _____
   _____

2. Into which shoes do you need to step to move forward in this area of your life?
   _____

3. Out of which shoes do you need to step that hold you back?
   _____

4. What is the one step you can take today to move forward?
   _____

5. Your life resolution for today:
   "I commit to (action) _____ today, as I move closer to experiencing _____ in my life!"

6. With whom will you share today's life resolution to help hold you accountable?
   _____

EVENING REFLECTION:

Which insights will you take into tomorrow?
_____
_____

Day 293

The more we feed ourselves with simple acts of kindness,
the more kindness grows within us.
We nourish our souls. Today, be kind to you!

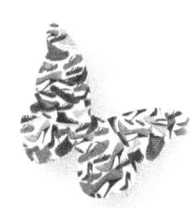

MORNING REFLECTION: Date: _____

1. What is your reflection from today's quote?

2. Into which shoes do you need to step to move forward in this area of your life?

3. Out of which shoes do you need to step that hold you back?

4. What is the one step you can take today to move forward?

5. Your life resolution for today:
   "I commit to (action) _____ today, as I move closer to experiencing _____ in my life!"

6. With whom will you share today's life resolution to help hold you accountable?

EVENING REFLECTION:

Which insights will you take into tomorrow?

Day 294

Our efforts can be infinitely multiplied when we care enough to act for each other. Today, multiply your efforts!

MORNING REFLECTION: Date: _____

1. What is your reflection from today's quote?
   _____
   _____

2. Into which shoes do you need to step to move forward in this area of your life?
   _____
   _____

3. Out of which shoes do you need to step that hold you back?
   _____
   _____

4. What is the one step you can take today to move forward?
   _____
   _____

5. Your life resolution for today:
   "I commit to (action) _____ today, as I move closer to experiencing _____ in my life!"

6. With whom will you share today's life resolution to help hold you accountable?
   _____

EVENING REFLECTION:

Which insights will you take into tomorrow?
_____
_____

Day 295

Every day, we can step into magical moments that allow goosebumps to evoke our senses and bring us closer to humanity and closer to ourselves. Today, feel goosebumps!

MORNING REFLECTION: Date:

1. What is your reflection from today's quote?

2. Into which shoes do you need to step to move forward in this area of your life?

3. Out of which shoes do you need to step that hold you back?

4. What is the one step you can take today to move forward?

5. Your life resolution for today:
   "I commit to (action) _____ today, as I move closer to experiencing _____ in my life!"

6. With whom will you share today's life resolution to help hold you accountable?

EVENING REFLECTION:

Which insights will you take into tomorrow?

Day 296

Belief is a choice, and when we choose to believe, we have all the power we need. Today, choose to believe in the power of your greatest self!

MORNING REFLECTION:　　　　　　　　Date:

1. What is your reflection from today's quote?

2. Into which shoes do you need to step to move forward in this area of your life?

3. Out of which shoes do you need to step that hold you back?

4. What is the one step you can take today to move forward?

5. Your life resolution for today:
   "I commit to (action) _____ today, as I move closer to experiencing _____ in my life!"

6. With whom will you share today's life resolution to help hold you accountable?

EVENING REFLECTION:

Which insights will you take into tomorrow?

Day 297

On the steps of opportunity, we can wait, or we can take the step to transition to the other side. Today, leap onto the steps of opportunity!

MORNING REFLECTION: Date:

1. What is your reflection from today's quote?

2. Into which shoes do you need to step to move forward in this area of your life?

3. Out of which shoes do you need to step that hold you back?

4. What is the one step you can take today to move forward?

5. Your life resolution for today:
   "I commit to (action) _____ today, as I move closer to experiencing _____ in my life!"

6. With whom will you share today's life resolution to help hold you accountable?

EVENING REFLECTION:

Which insights will you take into tomorrow?

Day 298

Our common pursuit, as human spirits, is to set ourselves free from whatever chains are holding us, and to soar. Today, set yourself free. Help to set another free!

MORNING REFLECTION: Date: _____

1. What is your reflection from today's quote?
   _____
   _____

2. Into which shoes do you need to step to move forward in this area of your life?
   _____
   _____

3. Out of which shoes do you need to step that hold you back?
   _____
   _____

4. What is the one step you can take today to move forward?
   _____
   _____

5. Your life resolution for today:
   "I commit to (action) _____ today, as I move closer to experiencing _____ in my life!"

6. With whom will you share today's life resolution to help hold you accountable?
   _____

EVENING REFLECTION:

Which insights will you take into tomorrow?
_____
_____

Day 299

*Our opportunity to use this life well,
to spend this day well, is all in the present moment.
It is now. It is here. Today, spend this day well!*

MORNING REFLECTION: Date: _____

1. What is your reflection from today's quote?

2. Into which shoes do you need to step to move forward in this area of your life?

3. Out of which shoes do you need to step that hold you back?

4. What is the one step you can take today to move forward?

5. Your life resolution for today:
   "I commit to (action) _____ today, as I move closer to experiencing _____ in my life!"

6. With whom will you share today's life resolution to help hold you accountable?

EVENING REFLECTION:

Which insights will you take into tomorrow?

Day 300

We only remain locked out of happiness until we come to see that only we hold the key to our greatest, most abundant, most purposeful selves. Today, unlock your happiness!

MORNING REFLECTION: Date: _____

1. What is your reflection from today's quote?

2. Into which shoes do you need to step to move forward in this area of your life?

3. Out of which shoes do you need to step that hold you back?

4. What is the one step you can take today to move forward?

5. Your life resolution for today:
   "I commit to (action) _____ today, as I move closer to experiencing _____ in my life!"

6. With whom will you share today's life resolution to help hold you accountable?

EVENING REFLECTION:

Which insights will you take into tomorrow?

Day 301

Each day we can unwrap all of the extraordinary gifts we have within us—we can discover and become our most gifted, powerful, and purposeful selves. Today, unwrap the gift of your greatest self!

MORNING REFLECTION: Date: _____

1. What is your reflection from today's quote?

2. Into which shoes do you need to step to move forward in this area of your life?

3. Out of which shoes do you need to step that hold you back?

4. What is the one step you can take today to move forward?

5. Your life resolution for today:
   "I commit to (action) _____ today, as I move closer to experiencing _____ in my life!"

6. With whom will you share today's life resolution to help hold you accountable?

EVENING REFLECTION:

Which insights will you take into tomorrow?

Day 302

When we reveal our treasures and allow them to shine through the surface, we cast our magic into the world. We illuminate our lives. We create light for others. Today, cast your magic into the world!

MORNING REFLECTION: Date: _____

1. What is your reflection from today's quote?

2. Into which shoes do you need to step to move forward in this area of your life?

3. Out of which shoes do you need to step that hold you back?

4. What is the one step you can take today to move forward?

5. Your life resolution for today:
   "I commit to (action) _____ today, as I move closer to experiencing _____ in my life!"

6. With whom will you share today's life resolution to help hold you accountable?

EVENING REFLECTION:

Which insights will you take into tomorrow?

Day 303

Our every step begins with a single thought, and a single thought can change our world. Today, think a single powerful thought!

MORNING REFLECTION: Date: _____

1. What is your reflection from today's quote?

2. Into which shoes do you need to step to move forward in this area of your life?

3. Out of which shoes do you need to step that hold you back?

4. What is the one step you can take today to move forward?

5. Your life resolution for today:
   "I commit to (action) _____ today, as I move closer to experiencing _____ in my life!"

6. With whom will you share today's life resolution to help hold you accountable?

EVENING REFLECTION:

Which insights will you take into tomorrow?

Day 304

When we choose to create our most powerful presence in each moment, we allow ourselves to soar beyond our limits. Today, soar beyond your limits!

MORNING REFLECTION: Date: _____

1. What is your reflection from today's quote?

2. Into which shoes do you need to step to move forward in this area of your life?

3. Out of which shoes do you need to step that hold you back?

4. What is the one step you can take today to move forward?

5. Your life resolution for today:
   "I commit to (action) _____ today, as I move closer to experiencing _____ in my life!"

6. With whom will you share today's life resolution to help hold you accountable?

EVENING REFLECTION:

Which insights will you take into tomorrow?

Day 305

The more we move mountains for others, the more mountains we will be able to move for ourselves. We will realize that our unlimited power becomes greater when we extend it to others. Today, extend your power!

MORNING REFLECTION: Date:

1. What is your reflection from today's quote?

2. Into which shoes do you need to step to move forward in this area of your life?

3. Out of which shoes do you need to step that hold you back?

4. What is the one step you can take today to move forward?

5. Your life resolution for today:
   "I commit to (action) _____ today, as I move closer to experiencing _____ in my life!"

6. With whom will you share today's life resolution to help hold you accountable?

EVENING REFLECTION:

Which insights will you take into tomorrow?

Day 306

Sometimes we will end up in the wrong place. There is no escaping it. So, we can either stay and be miserable, or kick ourselves in the pants, and tell ourselves to move on. Today, give yourself a kick in the pants!

MORNING REFLECTION: Date: _____

1. What is your reflection from today's quote?
   _____
   _____

2. Into which shoes do you need to step to move forward in this area of your life?
   _____
   _____

3. Out of which shoes do you need to step that hold you back?
   _____
   _____

4. What is the one step you can take today to move forward?
   _____
   _____

5. Your life resolution for today:
   "I commit to (action) _____ today, as I move closer to experiencing _____ in my life!"

6. With whom will you share today's life resolution to help hold you accountable?
   _____

EVENING REFLECTION:

Which insights will you take into tomorrow?
_____
_____

Day 307

You can close your eyes, feel the depths of your soul,
and let your spirit soar. Today, close your eyes and soar!

MORNING REFLECTION: Date: _____

1. What is your reflection from today's quote?
   _____
   _____

2. Into which shoes do you need to step to move forward in this area of your life?
   _____
   _____

3. Out of which shoes do you need to step that hold you back?
   _____
   _____

4. What is the one step you can take today to move forward?
   _____
   _____

5. Your life resolution for today:
   "I commit to (action) _____ today, as I
   move closer to experiencing _____ in my life!"

6. With whom will you share today's life resolution to help hold you accountable?
   _____

EVENING REFLECTION:

Which insights will you take into tomorrow?
_____
_____

Day 308

We each have the opportunity to create our own stage—to tap into our unique talents, our distinctiveness, and the passions that lie within. Today, create your stage!

MORNING REFLECTION: Date:

1. What is your reflection from today's quote?

2. Into which shoes do you need to step to move forward in this area of your life?

3. Out of which shoes do you need to step that hold you back?

4. What is the one step you can take today to move forward?

5. Your life resolution for today:
   "I commit to (action) _____ today, as I move closer to experiencing _____ in my life!"

6. With whom will you share today's life resolution to help hold you accountable?

EVENING REFLECTION:

Which insights will you take into tomorrow?

Day 309

In our busyness, it is easy to miss the magic in each moment—to move so quickly that we don't pause to experience the connection to all that is around and within. Today, pause and experience the magic.

MORNING REFLECTION:　　　　　　　　Date:

1. What is your reflection from today's quote?

2. Into which shoes do you need to step to move forward in this area of your life?

3. Out of which shoes do you need to step that hold you back?

4. What is the one step you can take today to move forward?

5. Your life resolution for today:
   "I commit to (action) _____ today, as I move closer to experiencing _____ in my life!"

6. With whom will you share today's life resolution to help hold you accountable?

EVENING REFLECTION:

Which insights will you take into tomorrow?

Day 310

The only way to grow on your journey is through people. Today, open yourself to another.

MORNING REFLECTION: Date: _____

1. What is your reflection from today's quote?
   _____
   _____

2. Into which shoes do you need to step to move forward in this area of your life?
   _____
   _____

3. Out of which shoes do you need to step that hold you back?
   _____
   _____

4. What is the one step you can take today to move forward?
   _____
   _____

5. Your life resolution for today:
   "I commit to (action) _____ today, as I move closer to experiencing _____ in my life!"

6. With whom will you share today's life resolution to help hold you accountable?
   _____

EVENING REFLECTION:

Which insights will you take into tomorrow?
_____
_____

Day 311

We forget that we are the ones who can create the "right" moment—by simply pausing and unwrapping the gift of the present moment. Today, pause. Unwrap the gift of the moment. Sit with it. Play with it. Be abundant in its presence.

MORNING REFLECTION: Date: _____

1. What is your reflection from today's quote?

2. Into which shoes do you need to step to move forward in this area of your life?

3. Out of which shoes do you need to step that hold you back?

4. What is the one step you can take today to move forward?

5. Your life resolution for today:
   "I commit to (action) _____ today, as I move closer to experiencing _____ in my life!"

6. With whom will you share today's life resolution to help hold you accountable?

EVENING REFLECTION:

Which insights will you take into tomorrow?

Day 312

Stepping out is uncomfortable, yet it is also exhilarating.
It is unknown, yet it is a gateway to freedom.
Today, be exhilarated!

MORNING REFLECTION: Date:

1. What is your reflection from today's quote?

2. Into which shoes do you need to step to move forward in this area of your life?

3. Out of which shoes do you need to step that hold you back?

4. What is the one step you can take today to move forward?

5. Your life resolution for today:
   "I commit to (action) _____ today, as I move closer to experiencing _____ in my life!"

6. With whom will you share today's life resolution to help hold you accountable?

EVENING REFLECTION:

Which insights will you take into tomorrow?

Day 313

We can't begin to find ourselves if we are lost, consumed, and paralyzed by pain and fear. Today, love yourself enough to step out of the pain and fear that hold you back.

MORNING REFLECTION: Date: _____

1. What is your reflection from today's quote?

2. Into which shoes do you need to step to move forward in this area of your life?

3. Out of which shoes do you need to step that hold you back?

4. What is the one step you can take today to move forward?

5. Your life resolution for today:
   "I commit to (action) _____ today, as I move closer to experiencing _____ in my life!"

6. With whom will you share today's life resolution to help hold you accountable?

EVENING REFLECTION:

Which insights will you take into tomorrow?

Day 314

We are our own directors, our own artists, our own playwrights.
Today, take charge of your story and choose to create all you imagine!

MORNING REFLECTION: Date: _____

1. What is your reflection from today's quote?

2. Into which shoes do you need to step to move forward in this area of your life?

3. Out of which shoes do you need to step that hold you back?

4. What is the one step you can take today to move forward?

5. Your life resolution for today:
   "I commit to (action) _____ today, as I move closer to experiencing _____ in my life!"

6. With whom will you share today's life resolution to help hold you accountable?

EVENING REFLECTION:

Which insights will you take into tomorrow?

Day 315

What if the things that brought the most back to us were
the simplest things we gave? Today, simply give.

MORNING REFLECTION: Date: _____

1. What is your reflection from today's quote?
   _____
   _____

2. Into which shoes do you need to step to move forward in this area of your life?
   _____
   _____

3. Out of which shoes do you need to step that hold you back?
   _____
   _____

4. What is the one step you can take today to move forward?
   _____
   _____

5. Your life resolution for today:
   "I commit to (action) _____ today, as I
   move closer to experiencing _____ in my life!"

6. With whom will you share today's life resolution to help hold you accountable?
   _____

EVENING REFLECTION:

Which insights will you take into tomorrow?
_____
_____

Day 316

Life becomes illuminated when we let life in.
Today, open yourself to life!

MORNING REFLECTION: Date: _____

1. What is your reflection from today's quote?

2. Into which shoes do you need to step to move forward in this area of your life?

3. Out of which shoes do you need to step that hold you back?

4. What is the one step you can take today to move forward?

5. Your life resolution for today:
   "I commit to (action) _____ today, as I move closer to experiencing _____ in my life!"

6. With whom will you share today's life resolution to help hold you accountable?

EVENING REFLECTION:

Which insights will you take into tomorrow?

Day 317

In this moment, we have the opportunity to pause, unpack, and repack all that we carry in our lives. It can be that simple. Stopping. Pausing. Making the choices. Today, pause, unpack, repack!

MORNING REFLECTION: Date:

1. What is your reflection from today's quote?

2. Into which shoes do you need to step to move forward in this area of your life?

3. Out of which shoes do you need to step that hold you back?

4. What is the one step you can take today to move forward?

5. Your life resolution for today:
   "I commit to (action) _____ today, as I move closer to experiencing _____ in my life!"

6. With whom will you share today's life resolution to help hold you accountable?

EVENING REFLECTION:

Which insights will you take into tomorrow?

Day 318

We have a different pair of shoes we can put on with each new day. We can dare to take the steps to follow our dreams. Today, step into the shoes that will take you to your dreams!

MORNING REFLECTION: Date: _____

1. What is your reflection from today's quote?
   _____
   _____

2. Into which shoes do you need to step to move forward in this area of your life?
   _____
   _____

3. Out of which shoes do you need to step that hold you back?
   _____
   _____

4. What is the one step you can take today to move forward?
   _____
   _____

5. Your life resolution for today:
   "I commit to (action) _____ today, as I move closer to experiencing _____ in my life!"

6. With whom will you share today's life resolution to help hold you accountable?
   _____

EVENING REFLECTION:

Which insights will you take into tomorrow?
_____
_____

Day 319

We are growing in the garden of our lives.
Today, tend to yourself with your greatest care, and you
will blossom with vibrant color, season after season.

MORNING REFLECTION: Date: _____

1. What is your reflection from today's quote?
   _____
   _____

2. Into which shoes do you need to step to move forward in this area of your life?
   _____
   _____

3. Out of which shoes do you need to step that hold you back?
   _____
   _____

4. What is the one step you can take today to move forward?
   _____
   _____

5. Your life resolution for today:
   "I commit to (action) _____ today, as I
   move closer to experiencing _____ in my life!"

6. With whom will you share today's life resolution to help hold you accountable?
   _____

EVENING REFLECTION:

Which insights will you take into tomorrow?
_____
_____

Day 320

We each hold the power to transform our lives,
to live our dreams, and to create the change we want
to see in the world. Today, express your power!

MORNING REFLECTION: Date:

1. What is your reflection from today's quote?

2. Into which shoes do you need to step to move forward in this area of your life?

3. Out of which shoes do you need to step that hold you back?

4. What is the one step you can take today to move forward?

5. Your life resolution for today:
   "I commit to (action) _____ today, as I move closer to experiencing _____ in my life!"

6. With whom will you share today's life resolution to help hold you accountable?

EVENING REFLECTION:

Which insights will you take into tomorrow?

Day 321

Know what you want, and then take it upon yourself to
make it happen. Today, take just one step to make it happen,
and another tomorrow, and another the next...

MORNING REFLECTION: Date: _____

1. What is your reflection from today's quote?

2. Into which shoes do you need to step to move forward in this area of your life?

3. Out of which shoes do you need to step that hold you back?

4. What is the one step you can take today to move forward?

5. Your life resolution for today:
   "I commit to (action) _____ today, as I move closer to experiencing _____ in my life!"

6. With whom will you share today's life resolution to help hold you accountable?

EVENING REFLECTION:

Which insights will you take into tomorrow?

Day 322

You need to be your best friend. Today, spend some time enjoying your own beautiful company!

MORNING REFLECTION: Date: _____

1. What is your reflection from today's quote?
   _____
   _____

2. Into which shoes do you need to step to move forward in this area of your life?
   _____
   _____

3. Out of which shoes do you need to step that hold you back?
   _____
   _____

4. What is the one step you can take today to move forward?
   _____
   _____

5. Your life resolution for today:
   "I commit to (action) _____ today, as I move closer to experiencing _____ in my life!"

6. With whom will you share today's life resolution to help hold you accountable?
   _____

EVENING REFLECTION:

Which insights will you take into tomorrow?
_____
_____

Day 323

The world can be full of hope and opportunity, or empty with fear
and doubt, depending on how you see it. Today, see it full.

MORNING REFLECTION: Date: _____

1. What is your reflection from today's quote?

2. Into which shoes do you need to step to move forward in this area of your life?

3. Out of which shoes do you need to step that hold you back?

4. What is the one step you can take today to move forward?

5. Your life resolution for today:
   "I commit to (action) _____ today, as I
   move closer to experiencing _____ in my life!"

6. With whom will you share today's life resolution to help hold you accountable?

EVENING REFLECTION:

Which insights will you take into tomorrow?

Day 324

When we give to others, we give to the mirror of ourselves. Today, see another as yourself. Give and you will receive.

MORNING REFLECTION: Date: _____

1. What is your reflection from today's quote?

2. Into which shoes do you need to step to move forward in this area of your life?

3. Out of which shoes do you need to step that hold you back?

4. What is the one step you can take today to move forward?

5. Your life resolution for today:
   "I commit to (action) _____ today, as I move closer to experiencing _____ in my life!"

6. With whom will you share today's life resolution to help hold you accountable?

EVENING REFLECTION:

Which insights will you take into tomorrow?

Day 325

We minimize ourselves with our doubt, and we lift ourselves up with our confidence. Today, talk yourself into your confidence, and fly high!

MORNING REFLECTION: Date: _____

1. What is your reflection from today's quote?
   _____
   _____

2. Into which shoes do you need to step to move forward in this area of your life?
   _____
   _____

3. Out of which shoes do you need to step that hold you back?
   _____
   _____

4. What is the one step you can take today to move forward?
   _____
   _____

5. Your life resolution for today:
   "I commit to (action) _____ today, as I move closer to experiencing _____ in my life!"

6. With whom will you share today's life resolution to help hold you accountable?
   _____

EVENING REFLECTION:

Which insights will you take into tomorrow?
_____
_____

Day 326

Don't let others bring you down. They only have the power you give them. Today, use your power to empower yourself!

MORNING REFLECTION: Date: _____

1. What is your reflection from today's quote?
   _____
   _____

2. Into which shoes do you need to step to move forward in this area of your life?
   _____
   _____

3. Out of which shoes do you need to step that hold you back?
   _____
   _____

4. What is the one step you can take today to move forward?
   _____
   _____

5. Your life resolution for today:
   "I commit to (action) _____ today, as I move closer to experiencing _____ in my life!"

6. With whom will you share today's life resolution to help hold you accountable?
   _____

EVENING REFLECTION:

Which insights will you take into tomorrow?
_____
_____

Day 327

Your life. Your terms.
Today, live your life on your terms.

MORNING REFLECTION: Date: _____

1. What is your reflection from today's quote?
   _____

2. Into which shoes do you need to step to move forward in this area of your life?
   _____

3. Out of which shoes do you need to step that hold you back?
   _____

4. What is the one step you can take today to move forward?
   _____

5. Your life resolution for today:
   "I commit to (action) _____ today, as I move closer to experiencing _____ in my life!"

6. With whom will you share today's life resolution to help hold you accountable?
   _____

EVENING REFLECTION:

Which insights will you take into tomorrow?
_____

Day 328

When others try to put us down, we must believe they can't. We are beautiful and divine beings. Today, allow no-one to put you down.

MORNING REFLECTION: Date: _____

1. What is your reflection from today's quote?
   _____
   _____

2. Into which shoes do you need to step to move forward in this area of your life?
   _____
   _____

3. Out of which shoes do you need to step that hold you back?
   _____
   _____

4. What is the one step you can take today to move forward?
   _____
   _____

5. Your life resolution for today:
   "I commit to (action) _____ today, as I move closer to experiencing _____ in my life!"

6. With whom will you share today's life resolution to help hold you accountable?
   _____

EVENING REFLECTION:

Which insights will you take into tomorrow?
_____
_____

Day 329

To fully experience love, we must reveal ourselves fully.
Today, reveal yourself.

MORNING REFLECTION: Date: _____

1. What is your reflection from today's quote?

2. Into which shoes do you need to step to move forward in this area of your life?

3. Out of which shoes do you need to step that hold you back?

4. What is the one step you can take today to move forward?

5. Your life resolution for today:
   "I commit to (action) _____ today, as I move closer to experiencing _____ in my life!"

6. With whom will you share today's life resolution to help hold you accountable?

EVENING REFLECTION:

Which insights will you take into tomorrow?

Day 330

Beyond your vulnerability is the truth of who you are—raw and real, ready to come into the world. Today, allow your vulnerability to leave you, and invite your true self into the world.

MORNING REFLECTION: Date: _____

1. What is your reflection from today's quote?
   _____
   _____

2. Into which shoes do you need to step to move forward in this area of your life?
   _____
   _____

3. Out of which shoes do you need to step that hold you back?
   _____
   _____

4. What is the one step you can take today to move forward?
   _____
   _____

5. Your life resolution for today:
   "I commit to (action) _____ today, as I move closer to experiencing _____ in my life!"

6. With whom will you share today's life resolution to help hold you accountable?
   _____

EVENING REFLECTION:

Which insights will you take into tomorrow?
_____
_____

Day 331

We can be our greatest advocates or our greatest enemies with the thoughts we have, the words we speak, and the actions we take. Today, be your greatest advocate.

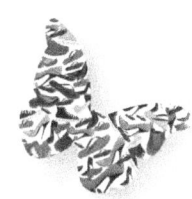

MORNING REFLECTION: Date: _____

1. What is your reflection from today's quote?

2. Into which shoes do you need to step to move forward in this area of your life?

3. Out of which shoes do you need to step that hold you back?

4. What is the one step you can take today to move forward?

5. Your life resolution for today:
   "I commit to (action) _____ today, as I move closer to experiencing _____ in my life!"

6. With whom will you share today's life resolution to help hold you accountable?

EVENING REFLECTION:

Which insights will you take into tomorrow?

Day 332

You can let go of your past, or carry it with you. It is your choice. Today, decide what you want to carry with you, and what you want to leave behind, and do it.

MORNING REFLECTION: Date: _____

1. What is your reflection from today's quote?

2. Into which shoes do you need to step to move forward in this area of your life?

3. Out of which shoes do you need to step that hold you back?

4. What is the one step you can take today to move forward?

5. Your life resolution for today:
   "I commit to (action) _____ today, as I move closer to experiencing _____ in my life!"

6. With whom will you share today's life resolution to help hold you accountable?

EVENING REFLECTION:

Which insights will you take into tomorrow?

Day 333

From our deepest challenges come our greatest opportunities to rise higher than we knew we could. We have the power to rise and to resurrect ourselves. Today, rise.

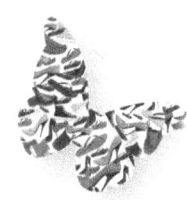

MORNING REFLECTION: Date:

1. What is your reflection from today's quote?

2. Into which shoes do you need to step to move forward in this area of your life?

3. Out of which shoes do you need to step that hold you back?

4. What is the one step you can take today to move forward?

5. Your life resolution for today:
   "I commit to (action) _____ today, as I move closer to experiencing _____ in my life!"

6. With whom will you share today's life resolution to help hold you accountable?

EVENING REFLECTION:

Which insights will you take into tomorrow?

Day 334

We cannot fill our lives with happiness if we do not allow ourselves to play and be lost in our passions. Today, lose yourself in your play and passions.

MORNING REFLECTION: Date: _____

1. What is your reflection from today's quote?

2. Into which shoes do you need to step to move forward in this area of your life?

3. Out of which shoes do you need to step that hold you back?

4. What is the one step you can take today to move forward?

5. Your life resolution for today:
   "I commit to (action) _____ today, as I move closer to experiencing _____ in my life!"

6. With whom will you share today's life resolution to help hold you accountable?

EVENING REFLECTION:

Which insights will you take into tomorrow?

Day 335

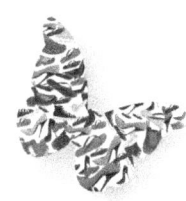

Within each of us are the gifts we need to fill our lives with abundance and happiness. Today, pause, unwrap your gifts, and bring them into your life.

MORNING REFLECTION: Date:

1. What is your reflection from today's quote?

2. Into which shoes do you need to step to move forward in this area of your life?

3. Out of which shoes do you need to step that hold you back?

4. What is the one step you can take today to move forward?

5. Your life resolution for today:
    "I commit to (action) _____ today, as I move closer to experiencing _____ in my life!"

6. With whom will you share today's life resolution to help hold you accountable?

EVENING REFLECTION:

Which insights will you take into tomorrow?

Day 336

Do not be shy of being great. That is your being.
Today, embrace your being and express it in your life.

MORNING REFLECTION: Date: _____

1. What is your reflection from today's quote?

2. Into which shoes do you need to step to move forward in this area of your life?

3. Out of which shoes do you need to step that hold you back?

4. What is the one step you can take today to move forward?

5. Your life resolution for today:
   "I commit to (action) _____ today, as I move closer to experiencing _____ in my life!"

6. With whom will you share today's life resolution to help hold you accountable?

EVENING REFLECTION:

Which insights will you take into tomorrow?

Day 337

We are all part of a greater force than we can imagine. Today, imagine the greatest you can be, and know you can be even more!

MORNING REFLECTION: Date: _____

1. What is your reflection from today's quote?
   _____
   _____

2. Into which shoes do you need to step to move forward in this area of your life?
   _____
   _____

3. Out of which shoes do you need to step that hold you back?
   _____
   _____

4. What is the one step you can take today to move forward?
   _____
   _____

5. Your life resolution for today:
   "I commit to (action) _____ today, as I move closer to experiencing _____ in my life!"

6. With whom will you share today's life resolution to help hold you accountable?
   _____

EVENING REFLECTION:

Which insights will you take into tomorrow?
_____
_____

Day 338

The universe offers us limitless opportunity, but we must be bold enough to step outside our comfort zones to let the universe know we are ready. Today, be bold.

MORNING REFLECTION: Date: _____

1. What is your reflection from today's quote?
   _____
   _____

2. Into which shoes do you need to step to move forward in this area of your life?
   _____
   _____

3. Out of which shoes do you need to step that hold you back?
   _____
   _____

4. What is the one step you can take today to move forward?
   _____
   _____

5. Your life resolution for today:
   "I commit to (action) _____ today, as I move closer to experiencing _____ in my life!"

6. With whom will you share today's life resolution to help hold you accountable?

EVENING REFLECTION:

Which insights will you take into tomorrow?
_____
_____

Day 339

Before us are many paths. If we are guided by our passion and purpose, the path we choose will lead us exactly where we need to go. Today, step forward with passion and purpose.

MORNING REFLECTION: Date:

1. What is your reflection from today's quote?

2. Into which shoes do you need to step to move forward in this area of your life?

3. Out of which shoes do you need to step that hold you back?

4. What is the one step you can take today to move forward?

5. Your life resolution for today:
   "I commit to (action) _____ today, as I move closer to experiencing _____ in my life!"

6. With whom will you share today's life resolution to help hold you accountable?

EVENING REFLECTION:

Which insights will you take into tomorrow?

Day 340
We are infinitely wise beings. Today, be infinitely wise.

MORNING REFLECTION: Date: _____

1. What is your reflection from today's quote?

2. Into which shoes do you need to step to move forward in this area of your life?

3. Out of which shoes do you need to step that hold you back?

4. What is the one step you can take today to move forward?

5. Your life resolution for today:
   "I commit to (action) _____ today, as I move closer to experiencing _____ in my life!"

6. With whom will you share today's life resolution to help hold you accountable?

EVENING REFLECTION:

Which insights will you take into tomorrow?

Day 341

Do not lose hope. The answer is around the
next corner. Today, turn the corner.

MORNING REFLECTION: Date: _____

1. What is your reflection from today's quote?
   _____
   _____

2. Into which shoes do you need to step to move forward in this area of your life?
   _____
   _____

3. Out of which shoes do you need to step that hold you back?
   _____
   _____

4. What is the one step you can take today to move forward?
   _____
   _____

5. Your life resolution for today:
   "I commit to (action) _____ today, as I
   move closer to experiencing _____ in my life!"

6. With whom will you share today's life resolution to help hold you accountable?
   _____

EVENING REFLECTION:

Which insights will you take into tomorrow?
_____

Day 342

The universe will do its work for you.
Today, ask for what you need.

MORNING REFLECTION: Date: _____

1. What is your reflection from today's quote?
   _____
   _____

2. Into which shoes do you need to step to move forward in this area of your life?
   _____
   _____

3. Out of which shoes do you need to step that hold you back?
   _____
   _____

4. What is the one step you can take today to move forward?
   _____
   _____

5. Your life resolution for today:
   "I commit to (action) _____ today, as I move closer to experiencing _____ in my life!"

6. With whom will you share today's life resolution to help hold you accountable?
   _____

EVENING REFLECTION:

Which insights will you take into tomorrow?
_____
_____

Day 343

In order to be great in the world, we first need to see the
greatness in ourselves. Today, see yourself for all you are.

MORNING REFLECTION: Date: _____

1. What is your reflection from today's quote?
   _____
   _____

2. Into which shoes do you need to step to move forward in this area of your life?
   _____
   _____

3. Out of which shoes do you need to step that hold you back?
   _____
   _____

4. What is the one step you can take today to move forward?
   _____
   _____

5. Your life resolution for today:
   "I commit to (action) _____ today, as I
   move closer to experiencing _____ in my life!"

6. With whom will you share today's life resolution to help hold you accountable?
   _____

EVENING REFLECTION:

Which insights will you take into tomorrow?
_____
_____

Day 344

We can be nice, and still not let people take advantage of us.
Today, draw lines with people who have crossed your boundaries.

MORNING REFLECTION: Date: _____

1. What is your reflection from today's quote?

2. Into which shoes do you need to step to move forward in this area of your life?

3. Out of which shoes do you need to step that hold you back?

4. What is the one step you can take today to move forward?

5. Your life resolution for today:
   "I commit to (action) _____ today, as I move closer to experiencing _____ in my life!"

6. With whom will you share today's life resolution to help hold you accountable?

EVENING REFLECTION:

Which insights will you take into tomorrow?

Day 345

You can stand at the control panel of your life.
Today, remove anyone else who is standing there.

MORNING REFLECTION: Date:

1. What is your reflection from today's quote?

2. Into which shoes do you need to step to move forward in this area of your life?

3. Out of which shoes do you need to step that hold you back?

4. What is the one step you can take today to move forward?

5. Your life resolution for today:
   "I commit to (action) _____ today, as I move closer to experiencing _____ in my life!"

6. With whom will you share today's life resolution to help hold you accountable?

EVENING REFLECTION:

Which insights will you take into tomorrow?

Day 346

Is your definition of success making you unsuccessful? Are you driven by your greatest passion and purpose from within, or by material things that will drive you to exhaustion? Today, define your success.

MORNING REFLECTION: Date: _____

1. What is your reflection from today's quote?

2. Into which shoes do you need to step to move forward in this area of your life?

3. Out of which shoes do you need to step that hold you back?

4. What is the one step you can take today to move forward?

5. Your life resolution for today:
   "I commit to (action) _____ today, as I move closer to experiencing _____ in my life!"

6. With whom will you share today's life resolution to help hold you accountable?

EVENING REFLECTION:

Which insights will you take into tomorrow?

Day 347

We are children of the universe.
Today, play with the innocence of a child.

MORNING REFLECTION: Date: _____

1. What is your reflection from today's quote?
   _____
   _____

2. Into which shoes do you need to step to move forward in this area of your life?
   _____
   _____

3. Out of which shoes do you need to step that hold you back?
   _____
   _____

4. What is the one step you can take today to move forward?
   _____
   _____

5. Your life resolution for today:
   "I commit to (action) _____ today, as I
   move closer to experiencing _____ in my life!"

6. With whom will you share today's life resolution to help hold you accountable?
   _____

EVENING REFLECTION:

Which insights will you take into tomorrow?
_____
_____

Day 348

We don't need all the answers. We only need to ask the right questions and listen for the universe to reply. Today, ask and listen.

MORNING REFLECTION: Date: _____

1. What is your reflection from today's quote?

2. Into which shoes do you need to step to move forward in this area of your life?

3. Out of which shoes do you need to step that hold you back?

4. What is the one step you can take today to move forward?

5. Your life resolution for today:
   "I commit to (action) _____ today, as I move closer to experiencing _____ in my life!"

6. With whom will you share today's life resolution to help hold you accountable?

EVENING REFLECTION:

Which insights will you take into tomorrow?

Day 349

Do not be anxious for what you do not have. Today, be excited for
all you have done and the unlimited possibilities before you.

MORNING REFLECTION: Date:

1. What is your reflection from today's quote?

2. Into which shoes do you need to step to move forward in this area of your life?

3. Out of which shoes do you need to step that hold you back?

4. What is the one step you can take today to move forward?

5. Your life resolution for today:
   "I commit to (action) _____ today, as I
   move closer to experiencing _____ in my life!"

6. With whom will you share today's life resolution to help hold you accountable?

EVENING REFLECTION:

Which insights will you take into tomorrow?

Day 350

You are your greatest gift.
Today, celebrate you!

MORNING REFLECTION: Date: _____

1. What is your reflection from today's quote?

2. Into which shoes do you need to step to move forward in this area of your life?

3. Out of which shoes do you need to step that hold you back?

4. What is the one step you can take today to move forward?

5. Your life resolution for today:
   "I commit to (action) _____ today, as I move closer to experiencing _____ in my life!"

6. With whom will you share today's life resolution to help hold you accountable?

EVENING REFLECTION:

Which insights will you take into tomorrow?

Day 351

If you have great intentions, you have all you need. Many have accomplished great things with nothing more. Today, so can you.

MORNING REFLECTION: Date: _____

1. What is your reflection from today's quote?
   _____
   _____

2. Into which shoes do you need to step to move forward in this area of your life?
   _____
   _____

3. Out of which shoes do you need to step that hold you back?
   _____
   _____

4. What is the one step you can take today to move forward?
   _____
   _____

5. Your life resolution for today:
   "I commit to (action) _____ today, as I move closer to experiencing _____ in my life!"

6. With whom will you share today's life resolution to help hold you accountable?
   _____

EVENING REFLECTION:

Which insights will you take into tomorrow?
_____

Day 352

You are a divine being, worthy only of praise.
Today, and every day, don't allow others to disrespect you.

MORNING REFLECTION: Date: _____

1. What is your reflection from today's quote?
   _____
   _____

2. Into which shoes do you need to step to move forward in this area of your life?
   _____

3. Out of which shoes do you need to step that hold you back?
   _____

4. What is the one step you can take today to move forward?
   _____

5. Your life resolution for today:
   "I commit to (action) _____ today, as I
   move closer to experiencing _____ in my life!"

6. With whom will you share today's life resolution to help hold you accountable?
   _____

EVENING REFLECTION:

Which insights will you take into tomorrow?
_____
_____

Day 353

There is no need to conform to what others want.
Today, allow your uniqueness to guide your actions.
Be true only to you.

MORNING REFLECTION: Date: _____

1. What is your reflection from today's quote?
   _____
   _____

2. Into which shoes do you need to step to move forward in this area of your life?
   _____

3. Out of which shoes do you need to step that hold you back?
   _____

4. What is the one step you can take today to move forward?
   _____

5. Your life resolution for today:
   "I commit to (action) _____ today, as I
   move closer to experiencing _____ in my life!"

6. With whom will you share today's life resolution to help hold you accountable?
   _____

EVENING REFLECTION:

Which insights will you take into tomorrow?
_____
_____

Day 354

Within us is the power and force to accomplish all we wish for ourselves. Today, wish big, and be your greatest power.

MORNING REFLECTION: Date: _____

1. What is your reflection from today's quote?
   _____
   _____

2. Into which shoes do you need to step to move forward in this area of your life?
   _____

3. Out of which shoes do you need to step that hold you back?
   _____
   _____

4. What is the one step you can take today to move forward?
   _____
   _____

5. Your life resolution for today:
   "I commit to (action) _____ today, as I move closer to experiencing _____ in my life!"

6. With whom will you share today's life resolution to help hold you accountable?
   _____

EVENING REFLECTION:

Which insights will you take into tomorrow?
_____
_____

Day 355

We are all part of a connected whole. With each action, we send a ripple throughout humanity. Today, send a ripple of positive change in your life and in the world.

MORNING REFLECTION: Date: _____

1. What is your reflection from today's quote?
   _____
   _____

2. Into which shoes do you need to step to move forward in this area of your life?
   _____
   _____

3. Out of which shoes do you need to step that hold you back?
   _____
   _____

4. What is the one step you can take today to move forward?
   _____
   _____

5. Your life resolution for today:
   "I commit to (action) _____ today, as I move closer to experiencing _____ in my life!"

6. With whom will you share today's life resolution to help hold you accountable?
   _____

EVENING REFLECTION:

Which insights will you take into tomorrow?
_____
_____

Day 356

Each day there are doors of opportunity before you.
Today, remember, you hold the keys.

MORNING REFLECTION: Date: _____

1. What is your reflection from today's quote?
   _____
   _____

2. Into which shoes do you need to step to move forward in this area of your life?
   _____

3. Out of which shoes do you need to step that hold you back?
   _____

4. What is the one step you can take today to move forward?
   _____
   _____

5. Your life resolution for today:
   "I commit to (action) _____ today, as I
   move closer to experiencing _____ in my life!"

6. With whom will you share today's life resolution to help hold you accountable?
   _____

EVENING REFLECTION:

Which insights will you take into tomorrow?
_____
_____

Day 357

Our intimacy connects us. Today, be intimate with yourself.
Then, be intimate with the world around.

MORNING REFLECTION: Date:

1. What is your reflection from today's quote?

2. Into which shoes do you need to step to move forward in this area of your life?

3. Out of which shoes do you need to step that hold you back?

4. What is the one step you can take today to move forward?

5. Your life resolution for today:
   "I commit to (action) _____ today, as I move closer to experiencing _____ in my life!"

6. With whom will you share today's life resolution to help hold you accountable?

EVENING REFLECTION:

Which insights will you take into tomorrow?

Day 358

Allow the color of love into your life.
Today, love those around you, and love will come.

MORNING REFLECTION: Date: _____

1. What is your reflection from today's quote?
   _____
   _____

2. Into which shoes do you need to step to move forward in this area of your life?
   _____
   _____

3. Out of which shoes do you need to step that hold you back?
   _____
   _____

4. What is the one step you can take today to move forward?
   _____
   _____

5. Your life resolution for today:
   "I commit to (action) _____ today, as I
   move closer to experiencing _____ in my life!"

6. With whom will you share today's life resolution to help hold you accountable?
   _____

EVENING REFLECTION:

Which insights will you take into tomorrow?
_____
_____

Day 359

A random act of kindness can change a life—including your own. Today, give one act of random kindness.

MORNING REFLECTION: Date: _____

1. What is your reflection from today's quote?

2. Into which shoes do you need to step to move forward in this area of your life?

3. Out of which shoes do you need to step that hold you back?

4. What is the one step you can take today to move forward?

5. Your life resolution for today:
   "I commit to (action) _____ today, as I move closer to experiencing _____ in my life!"

6. With whom will you share today's life resolution to help hold you accountable?

EVENING REFLECTION:

Which insights will you take into tomorrow?

Day 360

You can take yourself to new heights.
Today, spread your wings and fly.

MORNING REFLECTION: Date: _____

1. What is your reflection from today's quote?
   _____
   _____

2. Into which shoes do you need to step to move forward in this area of your life?
   _____
   _____

3. Out of which shoes do you need to step that hold you back?
   _____
   _____

4. What is the one step you can take today to move forward?
   _____
   _____

5. Your life resolution for today:
   "I commit to (action) _____ today, as I
   move closer to experiencing _____ in my life!"

6. With whom will you share today's life resolution to help hold you accountable?
   _____

EVENING REFLECTION:

Which insights will you take into tomorrow?
   _____
   _____

Day 361

With each moment of being, we discover something more authentic that creates an even greater being. Today, be in the moment.

MORNING REFLECTION: Date:

1. What is your reflection from today's quote?

2. Into which shoes do you need to step to move forward in this area of your life?

3. Out of which shoes do you need to step that hold you back?

4. What is the one step you can take today to move forward?

5. Your life resolution for today:
   "I commit to (action) _____ today, as I move closer to experiencing _____ in my life!"

6. With whom will you share today's life resolution to help hold you accountable?

EVENING REFLECTION:

Which insights will you take into tomorrow?

Day 362

Each day we can discover forces of good that enable us to conquer our demons. Today, discover your most powerful forces.

MORNING REFLECTION: Date: _____

1. What is your reflection from today's quote?
   _____
   _____

2. Into which shoes do you need to step to move forward in this area of your life?
   _____

3. Out of which shoes do you need to step that hold you back?
   _____

4. What is the one step you can take today to move forward?
   _____
   _____

5. Your life resolution for today:
   "I commit to (action) _____ today, as I move closer to experiencing _____ in my life!"

6. With whom will you share today's life resolution to help hold you accountable?
   _____

EVENING REFLECTION:

Which insights will you take into tomorrow?
_____
_____

Day 363

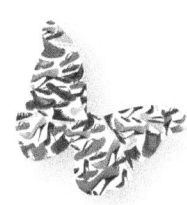

The only way to move forward is to keep moving with the currents, and feeling at home in the mystery and uncertainty that is an essential part of discovery. Today, move and discover.

MORNING REFLECTION: Date: _____

1. What is your reflection from today's quote?
   _____
   _____

2. Into which shoes do you need to step to move forward in this area of your life?
   _____
   _____

3. Out of which shoes do you need to step that hold you back?
   _____
   _____

4. What is the one step you can take today to move forward?
   _____
   _____

5. Your life resolution for today:
   "I commit to (action) _____ today, as I move closer to experiencing _____ in my life!"

6. With whom will you share today's life resolution to help hold you accountable?
   _____

EVENING REFLECTION:

Which insights will you take into tomorrow?
_____
_____

Day 364

Stop feeling guilty. No-one else is thinking about it anymore. Today, free yourself from your guilt.

MORNING REFLECTION: Date: _____

1. What is your reflection from today's quote?
   _____
   _____

2. Into which shoes do you need to step to move forward in this area of your life?
   _____
   _____

3. Out of which shoes do you need to step that hold you back?
   _____
   _____

4. What is the one step you can take today to move forward?
   _____
   _____

5. Your life resolution for today:
   "I commit to (action) _____ today, as I move closer to experiencing _____ in my life!"

6. With whom will you share today's life resolution to help hold you accountable?

EVENING REFLECTION:

Which insights will you take into tomorrow?
_____
_____

Day 365

You can change your life, you can change another life, you can change the world. It is your choice. Today, allow nothing to stop you.

MORNING REFLECTION: Date: _____

1. What is your reflection from today's quote?
   _____
   _____

2. Into which shoes do you need to step to move forward in this area of your life?
   _____
   _____

3. Out of which shoes do you need to step that hold you back?
   _____
   _____

4. What is the one step you can take today to move forward?
   _____
   _____

5. Your life resolution for today:
   "I commit to (action) _____ today, as I move closer to experiencing _____ in my life!"

6. With whom will you share today's life resolution to help hold you accountable?

EVENING REFLECTION:

Which insights will you take into tomorrow?
_____
_____

~ Your Journey Continues ~

I hope you have come far on your journey. Your journey continues with each new day.

You can use this journal again and allow each quote to move you differently and create new steps for yourself. You can find other quotes that inspire you to take new steps each day.

Whichever you choose, most important, is to keep finding inspiration, and to keep taking a step each day toward all you want for your life, and for the world.

Keep enjoying the journey, and keep sharing!

Find resources for your journey and ways to share at *www.ChangeYourShoes.com*

~ With Gratitude ~

Those who have helped me on this journey have been my life savers.

They have shown me that when you stay on your path of purpose, the universe will bring you exactly the people you need at the perfect time.

They have shown me that there is light beyond darkness.

They have shown me that the busiest people, such as Sheryl Sandberg, can make time to make a difference in the lives of those that they could easily dismiss. People like Sheryl give me hope and ongoing encouragement that in this sometimes overwhelmingly large world, we can each be seen, heard, and make a difference—something that can seem impossible when you have come from a background of abuse and isolation.

They have shown me that we are all each other's teachers and students. I'm grateful to Jack Canfield for nurturing the teacher and student within me.

They have shown me that love exists, that kindness can be exchanged between strangers, that extraordinary friendships are found in the most unexpected places, and that family are those who choose to embrace you as such.

Most of all, they have shown me that when we are brave enough to open ourselves to love, the real journey of transformation begins.

With thanks to all of you.

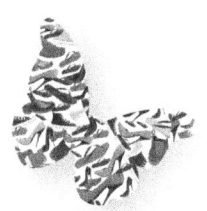

~ About the Author ~

Kathy Andersen left Australia to take a "break" that turned into a journey of a lifetime. Changing her corporate high heels to hiking boots started her on a journey where she would experience the power we each have to be our greatest selves and to live our greatest lives.

Among other things, Kathy's journey enabled her to step into the darkness of a childhood filled with abuse and isolation, and to step out knowing we are each so much greater than the worst that happens to us. She discovers the gifts and treasures waiting for each of us in every moment, and that with them, we can rise above any obstacles and soar to our greatest heights.

From traveling through some of the richest and poorest countries in the world, from remote villages, to shimmering cities, to wide open spaces, to ancient ruins, to sitting under the Bodhi Tree in India where the Buddha gave his first teaching, and even to the hallways of Harvard University, Kathy has discovered worlds within, around, and beyond that can take us on a journey to our greatest selves.

In her award-winning book, *Change Your Shoes~Live Your Greatest Life*, Kathy's journey took readers on their own journey of discovery. Now, in *Change Your Shoes~365 Life Resolutions*, Kathy provides a tool for each of us to take a step each day into all we want for our lives.

Kathy now lives in Miami Beach, and works to create positive change in the lives of people around the world through consulting, projects, speaking, seminars, workshops, and of course, writing.

In addition to Kathy's master's degree at the Harvard Kennedy School, Kathy has undertaken several executive education programs at Harvard Kennedy School and Harvard Business School.

You can follow Kathy on Facebook, Twitter (Kathy_Andersen), and other social media, where you will find quotes of the day and other messages to help you "change your shoes" and step into all you desire in your life and in the world.

www.kathyandersen.com

www.ingramcontent.com/pod-product-compliance
Lightning Source LLC
Chambersburg PA
CBHW060506300426
44112CB00017B/2565